TOP 20
Teens

Discovering the Best-Kept
Thinking, Learning & Communicating
Secrets of Successful Teenagers

PAUL BERNABEI
TOM CODY
MARY COLE
MICHAEL COLE
WILLOW SWEENEY

DESIGNED BY:
BRIAN CORNELL

ILLUSTRATED BY:
TIM PARLIN

SECOND
EDITION

TOP 20 PRESS • ST. PAUL, MN

Published by Top 20 Training
St. Paul, Minnesota 55413

First Printing: July 2003
Second Printing: January 2006
Third Printing: September 2008

To learn more about Top 20 Training or to order additional copies of Top 20 Teens, email us at: *info@top20training.com* or call (651) 690-5758.

Publisher's Cataloging-in-Publication Data
Bernabei, Paul.

Top 20 teens : discovering the best-kept thinking, learning & communicating secrets of successful teenagers / Paul Bernabei ... [et al.] ; designed by: Brian Cornell; illustrated by: Tim Parlin. – [Rev]. – St. Paul, MN : Top 20 Press, 2006.
An imprint of Morgan James Publishing
New York, NY   St. Paul, MN

p. ; cm.
ISBN: 0-9742843-0-0
ISBN13: 978-0-9742843-0-9

1. Success in adolescence. 2. Teenagers. 3. Teenagers-Life skills guides. I. Cornell, Brian. II. Parlin, Tim, ill. III. Title.

BF724.3.S9 B47 2006
158.1--dc22   2005910308

Printed in USA
10 09 08 07 06 • 5 4 3 2

"Discovering this book is the best thing that ever happened to me because it helped me succeed. It shaped me as a person."

— Whitney, Student

"I will not only use this information in my classroom, but in my personal life. This is valuable for all seasons... a must for all teachers."

— Colleen, Teacher

"After reading this book I changed. My parents noticed it immediately and our relationship improved. I now look at my life as a possibility, not a problem."

— Gracie, Student

"I've become the girl I've wanted to be."

— Nancy, Student

"This book and the TLC concepts help students learn life skills needed to succeed in high school and every day life. It has helped me as a teacher better connect with students as well as a father and husband at home."

— Pat, Teacher

"If I had to rank this book on a scale of one to ten, I would rank it eleven because it is unbelievable how much it has helped me and how much I've changed."

— Steve, Student

"In geometry you do proofs, in science you do labs, but in this book you learn the true meaning of living."

— Stephanie, Student

"I'm not the same quiet little girl who picked up this book. I am an assertive, motivated young woman who is not afraid of other people's opinions and raising her hand in class. I am more creative and willing to take responsibility for my actions. Thanks to this book and its principles I have bettered my best!"

— Allie, Student

Preface

Many authors are responsible for the creation of this book. Throughout our lives countless people young and old have shared their experiences, wisdom, and life lessons with us. Because of this our lives have been greatly enriched. The quality of our relationships, our education and our work have all been enhanced by what these "authors" have shared with us. They have enabled us to have a great ride through life.

This book is a tribute to their generosity and courage in sharing with us their life lessons, many of which were learned through struggle and sacrifice. We wish to express our gratitude for the difference their wisdom has made in our lives. And we wish to allow their gifts to also make a difference in your life.

Besides trying to live the concepts presented in this book ourselves, we have taught this material to students at Cretin-Derham Hall High School in St. Paul, Minnesota, in a course called **Thinking, Learning and Communicating.** Begun as a pilot program in 2000, the course has come to be known as **TLC.** The enthusiastic response of our students to this material has encouraged us to put this course into book form. We are grateful to our students, some of whom you will meet in the following pages, for validating these concepts in their own lives. They, too, are authors of this book.

All five of us work with young people ranging from our own children to students we have taught and young athletes we have coached. Our many years of involvement with young people have been sustained by their hopes and dreams. We know that a vast and wonderful potential exists in the hearts, minds and bodies of each teenager. We value our youth and believe they are not problems to be solved but potential to be developed.

The sole purpose of our TLC class and this book is to help young people, their parents and teachers develop that potential.

THE ORIGINS OF TLC

The development of the TLC course and the ideas in this book have evolved through the professional and personal journeys of five people.

Michael Cole's work with the concept of Emotional Intelligence began two decades ago. After a less-than-stellar academic career, Michael found himself floundering in the hair-styling business. His life changed dramatically when he met Joe Francis, who mentored Michael in the Emotional Intelligence field. He and his wife **Mary Cole** developed some of these ideas through their highly successful business, Salon Development Corporation.

The Coles first met **Tom Cody** when their two children attended Cretin-Derham Hall (CDH) High School. In 1996, the Coles approached the school administrators with hopes that their Emotional Intelligence ideas could be implemented at the high school level. At that time Tom, a math teacher at CDH since 1980, was developing "Jump Start," a pilot summer program for orienting incoming freshmen. The Coles' material was a perfect fit with Cody's practical study skills course. When the course outgrew the two-week summer program, it was introduced into the mainstream curriculum at CDH in 2000-2001 as a 12-week class called *Thinking, Learning and Communicating*.

Tom and **Paul Bernabei** had previously crossed paths as opposing girls' basketball coaches. Paul had been developing related concepts in his work as an educator and consultant. His work blended perfectly with that of the Coles and Tom. He joined the TLC team during its inaugural year.

Willow Sweeney, a CDH social studies teacher, joined the team a year later. She and Tom teach the classes on a daily basis. Paul and the Coles serve as guest lecturers and program developers.

This highly successful elective course began its sixth year in 2005. Over 75% of CDH students have chosen to take TLC. In addition, over 1,200 parents and 4,000 teachers have been trained since 2003. TLC curriculum is currently being used in over 100 schools throughout the United States. Trainings have been held from Boston to Boise to Honolulu.

ABOUT THE AUTHORS

Paul Bernabei directs Noble Ventures, an effort assisting schools, businesses, churches and organizations in developing their potential. He has been an educator in Twin Cities schools for 32 years, has conducted hundreds of retreats for youth and adults, and directs Share-a-Life, a program that provides housing and support for pregnant women in crisis. A graduate of St. John's University and the University of St. Thomas, Paul and his wife Paula, a kindergarten teacher, have four daughters.

Tom Cody has committed his professional life to education, serving as a grade school and high school math teacher since 1974. He has been instrumental in developing innovative curriculum programs at Cretin-Derham Hall High School where he has also coached several athletic teams. A graduate of Colorado State University, Tom and his wife Judy, a fifth grade teacher, have three sons.

Mary Cole is the co-founder and vice-president of Salon Development Corporation. For the last 22 years, she has developed materials, programs and products provided by her company. She facilitates training sessions with Michael, her husband and business partner. For the past three years she has been an adjunct faculty member of the TLC program at CDH. The Coles have two children.

Michael Cole has been a seminar educator for 32 years. For 22 years, he has been founder and president of Salon Development Corporation, an international company specializing in business training. He is a world-renowned recipient of numerous awards for his contribution in helping thousands of professionals transform their lives.

Willow Sweeney, a graduate of the University of St. Thomas, teaches classes in world cultures and social justice at Cretin-Derham Hall. Her specialized focus in TLC is on communication and relationship topics. Her exceptional ability to build rapport with teens helps make TLC relevant to their lives. Willow and her husband Brian live in St. Cloud, Minnesota.

As you read this book you'll discover what we have learned. Sometimes what is written in this book will come from us collectively and sometimes it will come from us individually in sections called "True Tales."

In order to avoid the use of "he/she", we have chosen to alternate gender pronouns.

TABLE OF CONTENTS

CORNERSTONES

The material presented
in *TOP 20 TEENS* rests
on key cornerstones:
The 80/20 Rule, **A New
Formula for Success**,
and **The Frame.**

These cornerstone ideas,
introduced in the first
three chapters, are woven
throughout the book.

They are essential to
helping you discover
the best kept secrets
of successful teens.

TLC
est 2000

The 80/20 Rule

When Michael Cole was 25, a mentor introduced him to the **80/20 Rule**, an idea that would eventually change Michael's life. The mentor told Michael that if he would just step back and observe people in life and what they are trying to do, he would find that **out of 100% of the people, 20% are making 80% of the difference.** The other 80% make 20% of the difference. That's not a bad thing. That's just the way it is.

What so powerfully impacted Michael was not that this was front page news, but that no one had ever said it to him that way. Michael immediately identified with the Bottom 80% who make only 20% of the difference. As a kid it seemed obvious to him that he was not lucky enough to be, nor destined to become, a Top 20. Michael saw himself as an average person.

"Before I took this class I had always thought that 80% of the population did 80% of the work."

– Kurt

This realization motivated Michael to ask his mentor the most important questions he had ever asked in his life:

"Who are the Top 20s and what do they know?"

"Can you teach me what they know and how to use it?"

"Is it possible that I could be a Top 20?"

His mentor's answer started Michael's quest. He said, "Not only is it possible, it is highly probable. I will teach you if you're interested and willing."

That got Michael going because he knew there would be many payoffs from becoming a Top 20.

Excited about this possibility, Michael wanted to get started immediately. His mentor's first lesson began this way: "We'll get specific but let me give you the big answer first. The single biggest difference between the Top 20 and the Bottom 80 can be found in a six-inch space between their ears. **Top 20s have a better way of thinking, learning and communicating."**

To that Michael asked, "Thinking, learning and communicating about what?"

"Everything," answered his teacher.

The point Michael's teacher was making was that the fewest number of people make the largest difference or experience the largest reward from their efforts. The greatest number of people make the smallest amount of difference. If you want to have a great life you have got to be a difference maker. The Top 20 make 80% of the difference, have 80% of the impact.

Generally speaking, it seems that:

20% of the Girl Scouts in any troop sell **80%** of the cookies.

20% of the students in class answer **80%** of the questions.

20% of the forwards on any soccer team score **80%** of the goals each season.

Becoming a **Top 20** requires that we improve our
THINKING, LEARNING & COMMUNICATING

STAGES OF POTENTIAL

What's really going on in people is that they're either developing their potential or they're not. This is true for individuals as well as groups: families, friends, teams, workers.

All people are in one of three stages of potential:

STAGE ONE
They're developing very little of their potential. Their negativity and false beliefs result in accomplishing far less than what they are capable of.

STAGE TWO
They're doing ok. They're pretty much meeting expectations.

STAGE THREE
Their potential is exploding. Because they've developed their potential, they're able to achieve far more in their relationships and experiences.

We call the first two stages the Bottom 80 and the third stage the Top 20. What makes the difference? It's simple. They **TLC** differently. Top 20s **Think**, **Learn** and **Communicate** differently than the Bottom 80s. That's what makes the biggest difference in what we get out of life.

Every person is capable of being a Top 20 or a Bottom 80. In every situation in our lives, we TLC in Top 20 ways or Bottom 80 ways. In fact, we might be operating in a Top 20 way in one area of our life and in a Bottom 80 way in another area.

WIRED FOR THE TOP 20

While all people have the potential of becoming a Top 20, not everybody believes they can or knows how to do it. One of the purposes of this book is to educate, empower and inspire you. **You have the potential of becoming a Top 20 and we are going to give you tools to help you realize that potential.** We want to help you eliminate your roadblocks—self-doubt, false beliefs, lack of awareness—holding you back from becoming a Top 20. The great news is that human nature has wired you to be a Top 20. We want you to discover the power that you've been given and how to use it to make a positive difference in your life and the lives of others.

Joe was a young man who graduated from our school. As a senior, he was selected as the number one football player in the nation. Joe was also an All-State player on our basketball team. To cap it off, Joe was the number one pick in Major League Baseball's draft and signed a contract to play for the Minnesota Twins. Besides being an outstanding athlete, he was also an outstanding person and one of the finest role models to come through our school. Through all his athletic success, he still looked out for the well-being of others. Joe certainly would be considered a Top 20.

HEADS UP!

We suggest that you not concern yourself with where you are going to be a Top 20 in your life. Rather, as you read this book, concern yourself with developing better Thinking (T), better Learning (L) and better Communicating (C). If you learn and apply what is in this book you will become a Top 20. It's not about becoming better at a skill or profession, although that might happen as well. It's about becoming **better at being you**. It's about the satisfaction that you will experience in developing your own personal potential as a student, a son or daughter, a friend, a person. Once you've developed your potential as a person, you are more apt to be successful in school, extra curriculars, or at work.

Being in the Top 20 doesn't mean that you will be able to throw a football, shoot a basketball, or hit a baseball like Joe. The world is filled with Top 20 opportunities, some of which you may not even be aware of yet. **It may be in medicine, firefighting, teaching or being a mother, father or friend.** In discovering the strengths and talents in your own personality, you will discover the areas in which you can be a Top 20.

As we go through the book we will continue to remind you that a certain way of thinking is the number one secret of the Top 20. We will show you how the Top 20 think about things and how the Bottom 80 think about things. You will see that the Top 20s' thinking is contrary to the Bottom 80s'. This doesn't make the Bottom 80 bad people. It just prevents them from getting out of life all that they are capable of getting. It prevents them from having a great experience.

STAR QUALITIES

Each of us is responsible for making his own life. We certainly have a lot of help along the way but we are the primary builders of our lives. As builders we all carry a tool box. Sometimes we may feel as though our tool box is empty and that we are not able to make anything meaningful in our lives. Sometimes it may seem that we have tools but we don't know how to use them. **The purpose of this book is to provide you with tools that will enable you to develop Star Qualities and create for yourself a place among the Top 20.**

What do you think makes the Top 20 different from the Bottom 80? When we first asked our students this question, they would say: "They're lucky" or "They're wealthy" or "They're born very smart or talented." In their minds there was some reason why others were in the Top 20 and they weren't. Students saw celebrities like Princess Diana, Julia Roberts, Tiger Woods and Bill Gates as Top 20 people. However, they didn't see themselves as being that lucky or that wealthy or that smart or talented. Well, let's get rid of that myth right off the bat. **There's more to becoming a Top 20 than just being lucky, wealthy, smart or talented.** When you reach the end of this book, you'll realize that you have all that it takes to learn the skills and develop the Star Qualities characteristic of the Top 20.

Star Qualities are at the heart of what this book is all about. Books and classes in school are usually about **information,** the giving or telling of ideas or knowledge. But this book is more concerned with **transformation,** the changing of your character for the better. The following are some of the most common Star Qualities.

- **Creative:** inventive, full of ideas
- **Self-Confident:** belief in oneself
- **Organized:** able to keep your life in order
- **Responsible:** willing to be accountable
- **Outgoing:** friendly, sociable
- **Self-Motivated:** self-starting
- **Persistent:** sticking with it
- **Enthusiastic:** having eager interest

- **Emotionally Aware:** in touch with feelings and thoughts
- **Self-Disciplined:** having self-control
- **Focused:** staying fixed on a goal or task
- **Optimistic:** hopeful, seeing the positive
- **Proactive:** doing what needs to be done before a problem develops
- **Courageous:** responding in spite of fear
- **Spiritual:** connected with your true self and your values

Although this is not a complete list, it is a list of qualities commonly found among the Top 20.

WILLINGNESS: GIVE IT A CHANCE

If you genuinely engage and participate in all aspects of TLC presented in this book, you will be absolutely delighted before you are half way through. You will be on the road to becoming a Top 20 and you will be getting more enjoyment out of your life.

What do we mean by **engagement**? We mean using the TLC tools that are offered to you in this book. So how willing are you to engage in this material? How willing are you to use these tools in the normal experiences of your life?

Take the example of Nick, a TLC student: "When I first started this class not only were my doors and windows shut, but they were reinforced with three-foot steel barriers. I didn't like the class and didn't think it applied to me. After a couple of weeks I decided to give it a chance. I definitely benefitted from taking the risk. There are so many things I learned from this material."

Nick's reference to his doors and windows comes from an analogy we use when presenting this material. Think of yourself as the owner of your own house (your thoughts, your beliefs, your value system, your decisions). Think of us as being in your front yard, at your front door, attempting to enter your home with these new ideas. It is completely up to you to decide whether or not to let us in. **Willingness is a major factor in this endeavor… and only you have the power to open the door to this process.**

"But," you might ask, " I'm already doing well in school. I'm doing all right in my life. Why bother with any of this?" We'll answer that question with one of the best kept secrets of the Top 20:

There is only one thing more important than being good and that is GETTING BETTER.

Bettering your best is important because, when you stop getting better, sooner or later you stop being good. And later always comes sooner than you think.

So you should probably stop reading this book if you **don't** want

- better relationships with your family and friends.
- more relevance and less boredom in your school day.
- a deeper self-understanding.
- as many happy days as possible.
- to become better at being you.

The University of Wisconsin has historically produced an outstanding marching band. This is a group that effectively balances excellent musical performance with healthy, fun-filled experiences. Their motto, one that we enthusiastically endorse, is quite simple:

You are now at a crossroads where a decision needs to be made. If you are willing to **push yourself** towards becoming a Top 20, then open your door and invite TLC into your life.

JUST IN CASE YOU MISSED IT

So here's the deal.

— The tools we are offering you in the following chapters are excellent tools for acquiring Star Qualities.

— If you are willing to use these tools consistently in your life, you will become a Top 20.

"This is not just about accomplishing goals, but about changing yourself. Change yourself and everything else will change with it. All those who have been successful had to work on themselves first."
— Justine

Is what we are promising too good to be true? Of course not!!! Many people are already on the journey.

How can we make these promises? First, we have observed Top 20 people and have discovered that they consistently use these tools. Second, we have observed many young people your age who have gone from the Bottom 80 to the Top 20 by using these tools.

READY...SET...GO

We want you to believe that **you** are capable of becoming a Top 20 by learning and applying these tools. Top 20s believe certain things; Bottom 80s believe certain things. The difference between these beliefs makes a huge difference in the lives of both groups, in their experience in school and relationships in life.

As you read each chapter, pay attention to what you believe about each topic. Is yours a Top 20 belief or a Bottom 80 belief? What's more important is having a Top 20 belief at the end of each chapter.

Are you ready? Let's get started.

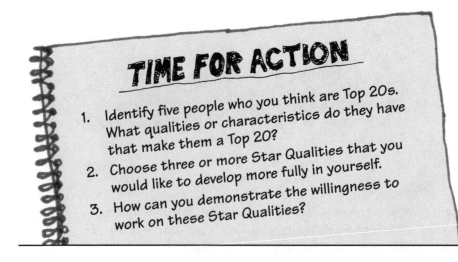

TIME FOR ACTION

1. Identify five people who you think are Top 20s. What qualities or characteristics do they have that make them a Top 20?

2. Choose three or more Star Qualities that you would like to develop more fully in yourself.

3. How can you demonstrate the willingness to work on these Star Qualities?

A New Formula For Success

Success is the feeling of satisfaction that comes from doing and being your best. We are not thinking of success in terms of money, grades, or popularity. Success means that you do not experience an unhappy teenage life, but rather have the most good days possible—**a good ride**. Success means that you accomplish your goals—**get good results**. In the process of your total experience you develop qualities and talents and become more fully who you are capable of being.

TLC focuses on three ways to attain success through

- better thinking which develops your "self-smarts."
- better learning which develops your "school-smarts."
- better communicating which develops your "people-smarts."

"My first part of high school ripped me apart socially and academically and lowered my self-esteem. I needed my Star Qualities back. TLC did it. I found my true self."
— *Jimmy*

THE BIG MYTH

In school so much of what is focused on is related to your IQ, your Intelligence Quotient. IQ means book-smarts, your natural brain power, which most people think is the major reason for success in school. You are usually graded and evaluated on IQ performance. Consequently, some students in the class feel disadvantaged. They don't think they have the smarts that someone else in the class may have. Therefore, they believe they can't be as successful. This is the BIG MYTH. IQ is not what makes the difference between the Top 20 and the Bottom 80. Rather, the biggest thing that separates the Top 20 from the rest is that they have developed their EQ, their Emotional Quotient.

Fortunately EQ is another way of becoming smart. EQ is becoming **self-smart**, **people-smart**, and a new way of becoming **school-smart**. A person can be successful in spite of not having a high IQ if they develop their Emotional Intelligence. The good news is that Emotional Intelligence, unlike Intellectual Intelligence, can be easily developed and improved. There is a debate in education whether or not we can raise IQ. In this book we are not concerned about that debate because we **know** we can wake up your EQ!

IQ and EQ can be compared to the wheels of a bicycle. The back wheel drives the bike and the front wheel steers the bike. The back wheel represents our IQ and the front wheel our EQ. Consequently, where we end up is the result of our EQ, our front wheel which is steering the bike. And it is this front wheel over which we have direct control when we grab the handle bars.

The concepts you will learn in this book are all intended to improve your EQ. Take control of the handle bars and steer your life in the direction you want to go.

THE ANATOMY OF YOUR EQ

Your EQ is made up of three important human characteristics.

$$EQ = \begin{matrix} \text{Thinking} \\ \text{SELF-SMART} \end{matrix} + \begin{matrix} \text{Learning} \\ \text{SCHOOL-SMART} \end{matrix} + \begin{matrix} \text{Communicating} \\ \text{PEOPLE-SMART} \end{matrix}$$

SELF-SMART	SCHOOL-SMART	PEOPLE-SMART
• Living with a positive attitude • Monitoring your moods and behavior • Improving self confidence and motivation • Bouncing back from adversity	• Finding relevancy • Eliminating boredom • Developing organizational skills • Making realizations • Getting into the Zone	• Getting along well with others • Listening and talking effectively • Resolving conflict • Becoming immune to negative influences

THE IMPORTANCE OF EQ

Let's see if we can better understand the importance of EQ by using the TLC formula for success: **Success = IQ X EQ.**

Imagine your IQ and EQ being on a scale of 1-10. If you have an average IQ of five and a low EQ of two, your total success score will then be ten.

Let's take a look at a few examples:

Example 1: Sally is bright (IQ = 8) and has her hand up all the time. She lacks friends because she is arrogant, boastful and irritates people. Sally doesn't have many people skills (EQ = 2). Her success total is only 16.

$$\underset{\text{IQ}}{8} \times \underset{\text{EQ}}{2} = 16$$

Example 2: Meanwhile, behind Sally sits Andy who has average brainpower (IQ = 5). Andy never gets any A's and struggles to get B's and C's. He is dependable, trustworthy and brings out the best in others (EQ = 8). His success total is 40. Notice that Andy's success total is more than double that of Sally's.

$$\underset{\text{IQ}}{5} \times \underset{\text{EQ}}{8} = 40$$

If Sally increases her EQ by developing some Top 20 skills and Star Qualities, she would improve the "ride" she is taking through high school and the rest of her life.

For many students there is a gap between their tested IQ and their GPA. In other words, many bright students are getting poor grades. Their IQ may be eight but they are performing as if their IQ is only four. By increasing their EQ, they begin to function intellectually at full capacity.

Michael is an example of this situation. As a student he did not have "school-smarts." He fell off the GPA/IQ Richter Scale. His naturally high IQ was stifled by his low EQ. When he took his college entrance exam he got to the fourth question and knew it was a lost cause. He finished the test by randomly guessing at the remaining questions. When his counselor talked to him about college, Michael was told that there weren't many options. He did qualify for two colleges: clown college and beauty college. Allergic to circus make-up, Michael chose beauty college. It wasn't until age 25 when Michael learned to apply the concepts in this book that he began to raise his EQ. His life then exploded into extraordinary personal and professional success.

When average IQ students become aware of this possibility they see potential for positive change in their own lives.

Yes, there is hope for you.
No, you don't have to feel
dumb or lonely anymore.

THINGS THEY NEVER TOLD YOU

An important part of life is problem-solving and most of life's problems are EQ related. We know that when adults fail in the real world it is not usually because they lack intelligence but because they are unable to work effectively with other people. This is even more true in our family life and friendships.

Clearly the front wheel is more important than the back. For people in leadership positions, EQ becomes even more crucial. Success is determined more by EQ than by IQ. But the paradox in our educational system is that the primary focus has been historically placed on IQ. In this book we are putting 100% of the focus on your EQ.

The secret we want to reveal in this book is that YOU have the power to raise your EQ. Therefore, YOU have the power to steer your bike towards greater success. YOU have the power to create a great ride with great results.

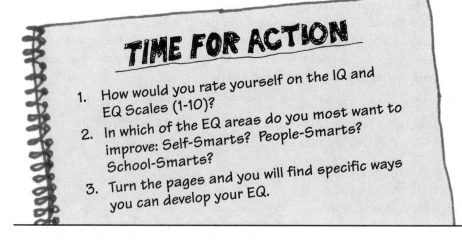

TIME FOR ACTION

1. How would you rate yourself on the IQ and EQ Scales (1-10)?

2. In which of the EQ areas do you most want to improve: Self-Smarts? People-Smarts? School-Smarts?

3. Turn the pages and you will find specific ways you can develop your EQ.

The Frame:
See-Feel-Do-Get

People have things in their lives that are important. What's important varies from person to person but for most teens the following are usually pretty important.

- Having a good relationship with family members and friends
- Having good health   • Doing well in school
- Doing well in extracurricular activities   • Having a job

Top 20s and Bottom 80s both want to get what's important to them. What is different, however, is that Top 20s know what to do when they are not getting what's important. They understand and use The Frame.

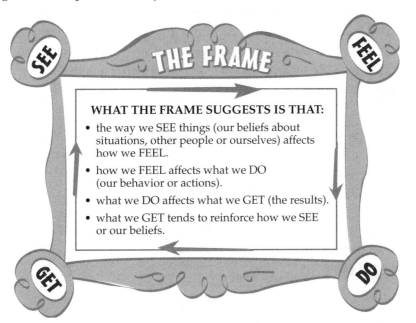

THE FRAME

WHAT THE FRAME SUGGESTS IS THAT:

- the way we SEE things (our beliefs about situations, other people or ourselves) affects how we FEEL.
- how we FEEL affects what we DO (our behavior or actions).
- what we DO affects what we GET (the results).
- what we GET tends to reinforce how we SEE or our beliefs.

So if you are getting what you want to be getting, if you are getting what is important to you, then you should keep doing what you are doing and keep seeing it the way you are seeing it.

But sometimes you are not getting what you want to be getting. You may not be getting the grade you want in your Spanish class, you may not be the starting point guard on the basketball team, or you may not have the relationship with your parents that you desire. If that's the case, what should you do that would make the biggest difference in increasing your chances of getting what is important to you?

BOTTOM 80 OPTIONS

If you're not getting what's important to you and you're operating as a Bottom 80 person, you have three options.

1. You could choose to **change nothing**. You would continue to see it the way you have been seeing it. You would continue to do what you have been doing and get the same results you have been getting. This pattern results in insanity. Isn't it insane to expect different results if you continue to see it the same way and do the same thing?

2. You could try to **change what you feel or do.** This might make a little difference in the results you're getting but it wouldn't bring about the big change you desire. Furthermore, the new actions would continue to present a challenge for you. It would always seem like hard work.

3. You could **blame** someone else or the conditions for the bad results you're getting. Bottom 80s almost always leave fingerprints of blame when they're not getting what's important to them. They blame a teacher for a poor grade or a coach for not getting enough playing time in a game. They blame the dog for messing up their homework or the weather for messing up their camping trip.

What happens when Bottom 80s blame? All people have power to make a positive difference in their lives. When Bottom 80s blame, they give away that power to another person or a condition. They then become a powerless victim unable to make a difference. They become **stuck in yuck**. They continue to experience the bad results they've been getting.

(Because it has such a negative impact on our lives, we'll be saying more about blame on pg. 72.)

TOP 20 OPTIONS

If you're not getting what's important to you and you're operating as a Top 20 person, you have a powerful option. You could be **CURIOUS**. You could think, "Wonder how I could see this differently." You could ask, "How can I see this person…situation…myself differently?"

Top 20s never give up power to make a difference in their lives by blaming. Rather, they expand their power to make a difference by being curious and seeing it differently.

As a Top 20 who understands The Frame, you know that by changing how you see, you will quickly change what you are feeling, doing and getting. Change in seeing gives you the possibility for big changes in the results you desire. Furthermore, the new action will seem more natural because it will flow out of the new seeing.

Let's use an example to see how this works. Imagine that your English teacher has assigned you to read a play by Shakespeare. The way you see this assignment will likely make a difference in the results you get.

"TLC helped me in my least favorite classes. I've learned to stifle my boredom and limit my distractions. I challenge myself to pay attention by seeing these classes differently. I've been feeling different, doing better work, and getting better results."
– Sophie

But what if you saw the assignment differently?

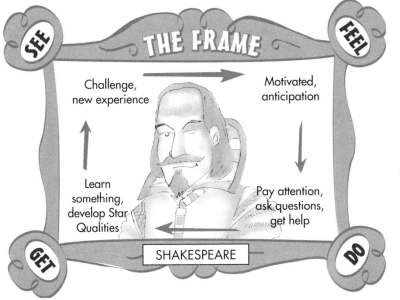

"I have a 90-minute class that's a big challenge for me to stay focused. I have started to SEE it as three 30-minute classes instead and it really helps pass the time and keep my interest."
– Nikki

"The Frame class completely and instantly changed my life. Now I relate almost everything I do to The Frame. It's my homemade insurance policy. When I don't know what to do, I take out a pen and paper and draw The Frame."
– Fred

Throughout this book we will refer to this change model as The Frame or See-Feel-Do-Get. It's a powerful tool by which you can look at situations and relationships in order to create a better experience for yourself and get the results you most desire.

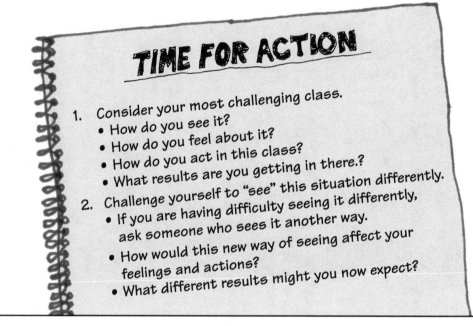

TIME FOR ACTION

1. Consider your most challenging class.
   - How do you see it?
   - How do you feel about it?
   - How do you act in this class?
   - What results are you getting in there.?
2. Challenge yourself to "see" this situation differently.
   - If you are having difficulty seeing it differently, ask someone who sees it another way.
   - How would this new way of seeing affect your feelings and actions?
   - What different results might you now expect?

"After school every day I do work-study and I would always see it as such a horrible thing and how I didn't want to do it. By the end of the day I'd feel lazy and not do the work as well as I should. Then my supervisor would tell me that teachers complained. So the day we learned See-Feel-Do-Get I decided to look forward to work-study. When I did that I did my work better and got compliments instead of complaints." *– Sara*

THINKING "SELF-SMART"

As a human being you have the wonderful ability to step outside yourself and examine who you are. By doing this you **become more aware: "self-smart."** You will learn important lessons which will empower you to experience life more fully and enhance the quality of your relationships. These lessons will enable you to develop Star Qualities (strengths) and avoid getting trapped in Negative Mental Habits (weaknesses).

As a result you will have more power and control of your life. You will make better choices as well as better manage your emotions and monitor your moods. Ultimately, you will become all you are capable of becoming.

You already have these powers within you. The purpose of this section is to awaken these powers.

Top 20s know that the biggest influence on their experiences is the way they think: about themselves, others and situations. The way they think is very different than Bottom 80s. Like Top 20s, once you become aware and take control of your thinking, you are destined for success.

This is an inside job first. It starts within you. It has nothing to do with people or situations outside yourself. So begin by taking responsibility for your own thinking and eliminate any blame, excuses or alibis.

The other sections of this book, **Learning** and **Communicating,** depend on you becoming aware and taking responsibility for your thinking. That's the first step in becoming a Top 20. Take that step by turning the page and reading this section.

An Inside Job

Let's start by thinking in terms of having two lives. One life is **the outside world**. This includes your life at home, school and work. But there is another world that we all live in—**the inside world.** It consists of the six inch space between your ears—**your thought life.** Your thought life is made up of your attitudes, opinions and beliefs about the outside world. These are all functions and activities of the inside world of your mind. So there are two worlds: stuff out there and what you think about the stuff out there.

What percentage of your success (good grades, good ride, good relationships) is tied to the outside, and what percentage is tied to the inside?

— The thinking of Top 20s is that most (90%) of their happiness or success is tied to the inside world and that very little (10%) is tied to the outside conditions.

— Bottom 80s believe just the opposite. They believe very little (10%) of their success is tied to the inside world. Instead, they place large value (90%) on outside conditions.

WORKING ON THE INSIDE IMPROVES THE OUTSIDE

Top 20s know they do not have control over the outside world but they <u>always</u> have control of their attitude about the outside. Knowing this and knowing how to use this can actually improve their outside world. **Top 20s use their inside world to influence their outside experience.** The person who masters this, masters life.

> 90/10 is the ultimate responsible thinking strategy.
> With 90/10 we eliminate our role of victim
> because it embraces the big belief: "I have power."

Top 20s' mission in life is to discover the power they have been given and then use this power to make their world a better place.

Think of a teacher with whom you might have some difficulty. Do you think it is easier to change your teacher or to change the way you think about your teacher? **Where does it make sense to put 90% of your energy?** Often we spend our time ganging up on the teacher and trying to get other kids in line with our thinking. All of this energy is wasted because the outside is usually very difficult or impossible to change.

A natural law of life states that **if you improve your inside you will eventually improve your outside.** Sometimes it may be sooner and sometimes it may be later, but it will happen.

BECOMING BETTER BY IMPROVING OUR THINKING

When we improve the inside, the outside eventually gets better. If you want a better team, become a better player. If you want to have a better relationship with a friend, you need to become a better friend. The first step of becoming is to improve your attitude about your team, your friend, and yourself.

You become a Top 20 by first improving your thinking and then by taking action on that new and improved thinking.

Thoughts such as "I totally disagree with this" or "I don't have a clue as to what you are talking about" will keep you firmly entrenched in the Bottom 80. Being clueless or resistant will not excuse you from the effect of this law. For example, if you don't like the Law of Gravity or disagree with it, that law will still apply to your life. Your choice is to comply with these laws and have a better ride or oppose them and experience negative consequences.

FREE TO DO THE INSIDE JOB

Accepting this law doesn't mean that life will never again deal us a bad card. We will still experience days when it rains on our parade. We will still experience the death or loss of a loved one. But even though we can't control those situations, a Top 20 still decides how she is going to operate in the midst of undesirable or painful situations. The belief in 90/10 recognizes an outside world that can often respond contrary to our desires or values. Nonetheless, Top 20s know that attached to every outside experience is an inside experience and **they have the freedom and the power to do the inside job.**

PAT'S RULE	Reframe the activity that you are not motivated to do into an activity that you are more motivated to do.

When Pat's mother asks him to vacuum the house, he reframes vacuuming to a more enjoyable activity. He will either start dancing with the vacuum cleaner or, being a football player, imagine himself in a game with two minutes to go. Quarterbacking his team in its "hurry up" offense, Pat times himself and tries to finish the vacuuming in two minutes or less.

Many times Top 20s are in a condition caused by the outside world. They can even be confused or stumped by this situation. They may not know what the better attitude is, but they know they're searching for one. They have faith that it exists and are open to the search. In their own way they are asking for a better perspective to have about this situation. For Top 20s that search usually results in finding a better way.

On the other hand, Bottom 80s believe that they are so victimized by the situation that they are powerless. There is nothing they can do to effect their experience of this situation. The outside has full control over the inside. It is hopeless unless the outside changes. It would never occur to them that there is a better experience available by doing an inside job.

> *"You will have more power to direct your life. You will have claimed the freedom that resides within you and will no longer be the victim you once thought you were. You will use the potential in your life now to create your future. You will even influence your outside world."*
>
> —Anne Frank

TRANSITION TO 90/10

We know that there are stages in life: infancy, childhood, adolescence, young adult, and adult. Teens are coming out of a stage in life where it is certainly not 90/10. For a baby or a little kid, life is more controlled by other people. This is necessary for the safety and well-being of a baby or youngster. During the adolescent transition period, teens should be taking on more control of their life by moving in the direction of 90/10.

However, because they have been in a dependent existence for such a long time, they may have formed the mental habit (belief) that that's the way it will always be. Top 20 candidates believe that that's the way it was when they were young children but, as persons who are evolving, they're always heading towards 90/10.

Do you believe this? Can you see yourself moving on the continuum closer and closer to 90/10?

Believing in 90/10 is fundamental to becoming a Top 20.

| 10/90 | 30/70 | 50/50 | 70/30 | 90/10 |

BLAMING, PRETENDING AND EXCUSE MAKING

"Bottom 80s blame. Top 20s tame." —Emily

Belief in 90/10 is not only powerful and liberating, it is also difficult. Accepting responsibility for our own life means we have to stop blaming others for our experience. Using the Blame-Thrower can become a convenient response because it gets us off the hook. Actually that is a false belief. It only appears to get us off the hook.

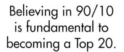

We also have to stop pretending that we have no control, even though we may have become quite good at that habit.

Pretending allows us to hide. The habit of pretending can be such a part of our everyday life that it is hard to stop. We can even become trapped in who or what we are pretending to be. Responsibility frees us not only from external controls on our lives but also from self-imposed traps of pretending.

Making excuses is an effort to protect ourselves. When we forget about 90/10, we use excuses like shields to deflect responsibility away from ourselves. Protecting ourselves from responsibility is a sure way of staying stuck in the Bottom 80. It assures us of not getting better and of having a miserable ride.

"Before TLC I was the king of all blamers. If I didn't score the goal, it was because my teammate didn't give me a good pass. I even blamed other kids for my own homework assignments. If I got a problem wrong, it was because Jimmy helped me with it."
— Sean

"Of course I'm not good at math...

...he goes way too fast and I'm always behind...

EXCUSE SHIELD

...plus, when I was in third grade I had Mrs. Johnson and she got sick in January and missed three weeks."

OUR THOUGHTS LEAVE FINGERPRINTS

The language of our thoughts helps us identify whether we are Top 20s or Bottom 80s regarding 90/10. Which of the following statements are you most likely to believe?

Top 20 Beliefs	Bottom 80 Beliefs
I use my attitude to control the event.	I allow the event to control my attitude.
I can always work on my inside.	I wait for the outside to change.
I'm not sure what it is but there's a better way of thinking about this.	There's nothing I can do. I can only do what I've always done.
I see choices.	I'm stuck.
Change is possible.	I can't help the way I am. It's in my genes...my family...and there's nothing I can do about it.

"After learning 90/10 I decided that I can still have a good day even when it's dark, cold and rainy outside."
— Charlie

Test these Top 20 thoughts by choosing to change your belief or attitude about something for one week. See if it has any effect. If it doesn't, you can always go back to your original belief or attitude. However, you might surprise yourself. You might find yourself saying:

"I didn't dislike him as much."

"The class didn't seem to go so long. It wasn't as boring."

You might even have a big realization: **"Wow, my attitude plays a much bigger role in my life than I would have ever guessed."**

LET THE PROBLEM BE THE PROBLEM

Certainly as human beings we experience problems in our lives. However, **the way we think about the problem can actually add to the problem**. If you are stuck in a traffic jam, that is a problem. The traffic jam is real. You need to get some place by a certain time and because of the traffic jam you are going to be late. So let that be the problem rather than creating others by allowing your thinking to go crazy and directing your rage at other drivers.

Maybe rain has canceled your baseball or softball game. Let that be the problem. But Bottom 80s will take that home and let the disappointment of the canceled game effect how they relate to their parents or siblings. Now they have more problems. Top 20s would do something like invite teammates home to play cards.

FORK IN THE ROAD

The remaining chapters in the **Thinking** section are all about self-smarts thinking tools. None of these tools can be activated, however, without accepting the 90/10 Rule. So we have come to a crucial fork in the road. The only way to become a Top 20 is to take Highway 90/10. This is the road to responsibility, empowerment, and taking control of your life.

"On my way to my least favorite class I'd be complaining how long, boring, stupid and pointless this long, boring, stupid, pointless class was. With that mindset I'd slump down and watch the clock hands seemingly move backwards. I was getting nothing out of this class and my D grade reflected it. Then it hit me. Why should I let these teachers control how my class, day or grades go? I don't want to give them my power. After realizing this, my class became much more enjoyable."
— Reed

It all starts here. What's your decision?

If it's gonna BE,
it's up to ME.

"I was at our cabin in the winter. I had nothing to do since it was freezing outside. But I decided to put on a hat and gloves and build a snow fort with my brother. It was a blast. I didn't let the snow and cold ruin my day."
– Harley

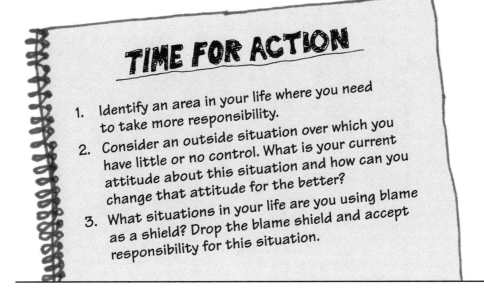

TIME FOR ACTION

1. Identify an area in your life where you need to take more responsibility.

2. Consider an outside situation over which you have little or no control. What is your current attitude about this situation and how can you change that attitude for the better?

3. What situations in your life are you using blame as a shield? Drop the blame shield and accept responsibility for this situation.

Do You See or Are You Blind?

So much of what we share in this book has to do with seeing: how we see, what we see, if we see, old ways of seeing and new ways of seeing. We'll begin this chapter with what appears to be a ridiculous question: *Do you see?*

Let's do an experiment. Read the following sentence carefully. We'll ask you a question when you've finished.

> **FINISHED FILES ARE THE RESULT OF YEARS OF SCIENTIFIC STUDY COMBINED WITH THE EXPERIENCE OF MANY YEARS.**

Before we ask you the question, read the sentence again.

Now that you've read the sentence a few times, count the number of F's in the sentence. How many letter F's are there in the sentence?

Look again and count the number of F's a second time.

Are you coming up with the same number?

When we've done this with groups of students, most have only seen three F's in the sentence. A smaller number would see four or five F's. Usually only 20% or less would see six F's, which is the correct answer.

If you didn't see six F's, you probably missed the F's that are in "OF." That's quite common.

"Before I heard this I was blind. Now I have new glasses to see through."
– Molly

What can we learn from the fact that most people don't see six F's in this sentence? People often don't see what is obvious. In this case, we don't see what's black and white. If we often don't see what's obvious, how can we be sure that we see (or understand or know) what's not so obvious, like what someone's motive is when he says or does something. Yet, we usually think we do know. Why? Because **we think we see things the way they are.** That's rarely the case.

PARADIGMS

What we are considering here are paradigms. **Paradigms are the patterned way we see reality**. They are the pictures we have in our head about the way things are. **Paradigms form our perspective**—the way we see situations, the way we see other people, even the way we see ourselves.

Paradigms are a powerful part of our lives. Because our paradigms are the way we see, they influence our emotions (what we feel) and our behavior (what we do), and, therefore, effect the results (what we get). Consequently, changing our paradigm, having a **paradigm shift**, will cause us to get different results.

When Paul's daughter Megan was three years old, he took her to a basketball game. During the game Megan fell twenty feet through the bleachers and landed head first on a cement floor. As Paul rushed her to the hospital, Megan's head was swelling as if someone was blowing air into a balloon. Paul thought that his young daughter was dead or dying. Although Megan suffered multiple skull fractures from this fall, she eventually regained her full health.

How did this event impact Paul's paradigm? A part of every father's paradigm is to protect his children. Because of this incident, protecting his daughter became even a larger part of Paul's paradigm as father.

This paradigm worked well as Megan grew through her grade school years. But once she entered high school, Paul's determination to protect her resulted in her resistance and rebellion. Paul became scared, angry and frustrated by Megan's behavior. After several months he desired relief from this constant problem and said to his wife, "I wish we didn't have her." As painful as that realization was, this was his true feeling.

At the time Paul was a high school counselor. He realized that the paradigm he had as father was very different from the paradigm he had as counselor.

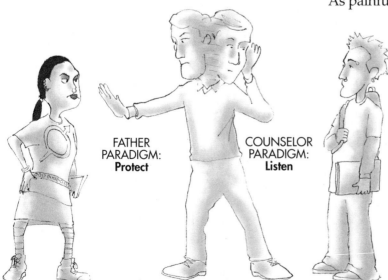

FATHER
PARADIGM:
Protect

COUNSELOR
PARADIGM:
Listen

The biggest part of his father paradigm was protecting and the biggest part of his counselor paradigm was listening. Paul decided to make a shift from protecting Megan to listening to her. After all, protecting sure wasn't working. Paul wasn't getting what was important to him—being close to his daughter. To continue to try to protect would probably get the same terrible results. That would be insane.

This paradigm shift caused Paul to see himself, Megan and the situation differently. Consequently, he felt and acted differently (more listening) and got different results (their relationship ultimately grew very close).

PARADIGMS ARE ALWAYS INCOMPLETE

Although the details of this story are different from your own experiences, your life and Paul's example share some things in common.

First, **we might hold onto a paradigm even when it isn't working for us**, even when we are not getting the results that are important to us. One reason we do this is because we usually think we are right. In fact, we may be. Paul certainly was right in having a paradigm about protecting his daughter. Most every father on earth would agree that that is a correct paradigm.

So why would you change a paradigm if it is correct? **You change if your correct paradigm is not effective in getting the results that are important to you.** You change because you are failing at what you want most.

Although Paul's paradigm was correct, it was incomplete. There was more to the situation than he was seeing, just like the sentence with 6 F's. Yes, it's true that on page 29 there are three F's in the sentence. Although that's correct, it's not complete. There are also three more that most people don't see.

It may sound strange to hear that Top 20s are blind, that their paradigms are incomplete and that they don't see reality exactly as it is. What about Bottom 80s? Well, they're blind too. The difference is that **Top 20s know it.** They know that their paradigms are incomplete and that they don't see reality clearly. As a result, they are more open to getting additional information. In fact, they seek it. Consequently, their paradigms are less incomplete than they would have been if they didn't know they were blind.

We need to learn this about all of our paradigms. They are never complete. We don't see anything (ourselves, others or a situation) exactly as it is. **If we know that we are blind, we will be more open to seeing what we do not see.**

"I was looking at life through binoculars, but I was holding them the wrong way. Learning about 'seeing' helped me turn them around."
– Charlie

PARADIGM SHIFTS

A paradigm shift occurs when we change how we are seeing something. If paradigm shifts help us see things to which we were previously blind, how can we get a new perspective? There are three ways to expand our paradigms and improve our seeing:

1. Create a Crisis. The purpose of a crisis is to bring about a paradigm shift. The Civil War was a national crisis caused by the belief that human beings could be held as slaves. The result of this crisis was that we began to see that this was not only an incomplete paradigm but also an incorrect belief.

Crises are very effective in bringing about paradigm shifts. However, the problem with crises is the pain and suffering involved (such as in the Civil War or Paul and Megan's relationship). While crises often work, it will be less painful if you use the other two ways to bring about a shift.

2. Ask Others How They See It. Who will see a situation differently than you? Anyone. No two people see anything exactly alike. So by asking someone else how she sees a person or situation, you will expand your paradigm and see it more completely.

3. Change Roles. We will automatically change how we see if we change roles. How does the situation look through your parents' or teacher's eyes, through your younger brother's or older sister's eyes, through the eyes of a person from a different country or race? Paul looked at his situation through the eyes of a counselor and saw Megan and what he could do very differently.

When Tom was coaching basketball, a player who wanted more playing time came to him. Tom asked her what she would do if she were her coach. As she looked at the situation from a coach's point of view, she said she would have her playing about the same amount of time she was already playing. Changing roles got her to see the situation differently.

4. Say "Maybe". Have you ever noticed trees growing out of rock? It actually happens. They can't grow out of solid rock but huge trees can grow where there's a crack in a rock.

The same is true for you. If you're rock-headed, if you think you're absolutely right about how you see something, you'll never see more or differently. You'll stay **stuck in yuck**. If you're convinced there's no point in reading this book, there won't be – for you!! If you're convinced a teacher doesn't like you, it sure will feel like that – for you!!

Top 20s know that if they put the word "Maybe" before judgments they make, they can create a crack in which something else might grow. If you say, "Maybe there's no point reading this book," you might find something valuable reading this book. If you say, "Maybe my teacher doesn't like me," you might discover something new about your teacher.

TWO PATHS

In every situation in our life, we can take one of two paths. This book will help you be more aware of these two paths. With that awareness you will be more able to choose the Top 20 path.

BOTTOM 80 PATH	TOP 20 PATH
I don't see.	I don't see.
Because I don't know that I don't see, I think I know and see everything exactly the way it is.	Because I know that I don't see, I know I don't know and don't see everything exactly the way it is.
Therefore, I'm RIGHT.	Therefore, I'm CURIOUS.
Then I BLAME.	Then I LEARN.
I lose power.	I see more.
I'm a victim.	I'm a difference maker.
I stay stuck in yuck.	I get a better experience.

SOLUTIONS OR BLAME

If we are not getting the results that we want and we are not aware that we are blind, the tendency is to blame others. Since we believe we see the person or situation correctly, it must be someone else's fault. Our blaming disempowers us and keeps us from making the situation better.

On the other hand, if you know you don't see the situation completely, your tendency will not be to blame someone else. Rather, you will take responsibility to expand your vision and will more likely improve the situation. **Top 20s find solutions; Bottom 80s find someone to blame.**

Do You See or Are You Blind?

You might begin to see more once you know you're blind.

THREE RIGHTS

Have you ever noticed how important it is for people to be right? Sometimes being right matters more than being effective or getting what's really important to us. When that happens, our need to be right can keep us from getting the results we want.

Let's look at three different ways of thinking about being right that are likely to pop up when we're not getting what we want to be getting.

1. When you think you're right, you're right. There are no other possibilities or options. There is no other way of seeing it. This is a Bottom 80 way of being right because it leads directly to blame. If you're not getting what's important to you and you think you're right, then someone or something else must be wrong. Since you're right, you can just blame them. In blaming them, you give up your power to make a difference and stay stuck in yuck. Doesn't that sound like a Bottom 80 experience?

When you start feeling the urge or need to be right, say to yourself, "**Maybe** I'm wrong. I wonder how I can see this differently?"

When you start feeling the urge or need to be right, say to yourself, "**Maybe** I am right **BUT** there's still something more I'm not seeing. I wonder how I can see what I'm not seeing yet?"

2. When you think you're right, you're aware that you might be wrong; you just haven't discovered what you're wrong about yet. Strange as it may seem, that's a Top 20 way of thinking. Why? Because it prevents blame and leads to curiosity. If you think you might be wrong, you won't blame someone else. Furthermore, realizing that you might be wrong means you might keep an open mind. You also might ask questions and listen more. Your curiosity might result in your seeing something more or different and create for you a Top 20 experience.

3. When you think you're right, you are right, but there's always something more that you're not seeing. This is another Top 20 way of thinking. Top 20s know they never see anything – other people, a situation, even themselves – exactly the way it is. They know there's always something more that they are not seeing. Therefore, they start with that thinking. When they begin to think they're right, they know that, even if they are right, there's still something more they are not seeing. Once again, thinking that way leads them to being curious.

What bugs Bottom 80s is being wrong. Their refusal to accept that possibility prevents them from moving on.

What bugs Top 20s is being stuck in yuck. They don't mind being wrong or not knowing everything. They know they always have the curious card to play. It's a winner every time.

TIME FOR ACTION

1. Consider a part of your life in which you are not getting what is important to you. How do you see yourself and other people in this situation?

2. Before a crisis occurs get a new perspective by expanding your paradigm.
   - Ask someone else how he or she sees it
   - Change roles

Beliefs:
Fact or Fiction?

Beliefs play a more important role in our success than most people realize. Have you ever noticed how athletic teams after championship games or seasons give credit to believing? "We believed we could do it." This is not a coincidence. **Believing is the beginning of achieving.** The reason for this is that beliefs impact how we see. They become the lenses through which we see reality. As you learned from The Frame, how we see influences how we feel, what we do, and what we get.

FACTS OR BELIEFS

Sometimes we confuse facts and beliefs. We may believe something so strongly or have believed it for so long that it begins to look like a fact.

— A **FACT** is something that is **true for all people**.

— A **BELIEF** is a thought or idea that **you think is true.**

Facts have their origin in reality. Beliefs have their origin in your mind as you try to match your thinking with reality. **The Law of Beliefs states that whatever we believe is real for us.**

Fact or Belief? It's too cold to go camping when it's 20 degrees outside. Yes, it may be cold but some people not only camp in the winter but love it.

Is the statement, "I'm stupid in science," a fact or a belief? Sometimes statements like this **feel** like facts. So we may draw the conclusion: "That's not a belief. It's a fact." We need to remember that our feelings stem more from our opinions and beliefs than they do from facts.

When beliefs are invisible, they appear to be facts. As beliefs become visible, we know they are no longer facts. We still may believe them. We still may hang on to them, but we hang on to them as beliefs and not as facts.

FACT
Water freezes at 32 degrees Fahrenheit.

BELIEF
It's too cold to go camping when it's 20 degrees outside!

FALSE BELIEFS BLOCK POTENTIAL

Many of our beliefs are based in truth, but some are not. The problem is that Bottom 80s usually think all of their beliefs are true and act accordingly. On the other hand, Top 20s question the validity of their beliefs.

"In sixth grade I had a hard time making friends. Being nervous, self-conscious and embarrassed, I believed no one liked me. I realize now that that was a belief. Today I believe differently and have made all sorts of friends."
– Emily

Whether true or false, beliefs are powerful in our lives because they influence us to act in certain ways. False beliefs have us acting in ways that are not in our best interest.

False beliefs diminish our lives. They hold us back and keep us stuck in places we would rather not be. Whenever we are stuck in a place we would rather not be, we need to search for the belief we have that is keeping us there. Usually there is one. A false belief can block us from seeing the truth because **we are convinced that the false belief is the truth.**

The purpose of beliefs is to enhance our lives. We hold on to beliefs because we think they help us get to a new and better place or help us develop ourselves and our relationships. This will almost always happen if our beliefs are based in truth.

LAW OF "I AM"

Another way to look at your own beliefs is to examine your self-talk. Consider how you finish sentences that begin with the words "I am".

Examples: "I am going to fail this math quiz."
"I am about to figure out this problem."
"I am going to be bored in school today."

Whatever you say after the words "I am" seems to set your immediate future in motion. Your "I am" statements usually come true. It is as if a magical genie appears from the bottle, ready and willing to grant your every wish.

I am NEVER going to understand this math!

LAW OF I AM
Whatever we say after we say
"I am..." is what we will become.

Most "I am" statements can be traced to one of the two major root systems that nourish your tree of beliefs. One root **limits your potential**. It is based in a deep belief: "I am not good enough." Bottom 80s are often unaware of this root even though it has a negative influence on their life and experiences.

The following are examples of "I am" statements that might stem from this belief:

> "I am not going to make the spring play."
> "I am never going to get along well with my dad."

The other root system **enhances your potential**. It is based on a different deep belief: "I am fully capable." Top 20s nourish this root and have more productive lives and experiences. From this belief comes "I am" statements like:

> "I am going to listen in science today."
> "I am going to enjoy this weekend with my family."

Be careful. Which of these two roots is influencing your life?

LAW OF CONVICTION

Your level of conviction is important because it will determine how real your beliefs feel to you. That in turn will determine the impact that your beliefs will actually have on your life.

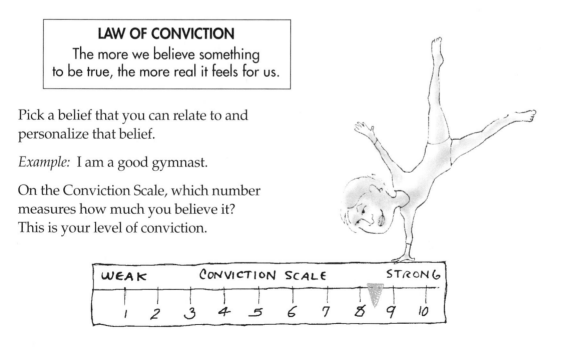

> **LAW OF CONVICTION**
> The more we believe something
> to be true, the more real it feels for us.

Pick a belief that you can relate to and personalize that belief.

Example: I am a good gymnast.

On the Conviction Scale, which number measures how much you believe it? This is your level of conviction.

WEAK   CONVICTION SCALE   STRONG

1 2 3 4 5 6 7 8 9 10

EASE UP

If you have a false idea in your head that you think is true, that idea will get in your way. An example of this is Carlos, one of our TLC students who believed that he was not smart in math: "I have never done well in math and I never will. I was born that way. It runs in the family. Every day I go into math class, the 50-minute class feels like three hours."

Carlos' conviction score on his belief about math was about a **10**. We asked him if he would be willing to turn down the conviction on his belief. We didn't ask him to abandon his belief but to ease up on the intensity of his conviction (to a **7** or **8**). Carlos was willing to reduce his conviction to a **7** by paying attention in class. He believed he could do this for three days.

When we checked in with Carlos three days later he said, "I can't believe what's going on in math. It doesn't seem as hard. There have even been a couple of times in math where I started to understand it. Class isn't as painful. It only seems like 50 minutes." Later, Carlos lowered his conviction from a **7** to a **4** on his own and his grade went from a D+ to a B-.

"Before TLC I believed my parents wouldn't let me grow up. I eased up from an 8 to a 5 on this belief and realized they just wanted me to be safe. My belief was false."
— Armin

A second example involves Anisa, a student who believed that her English teacher hated her. Her conviction of this belief was off the charts (**10+**). Due to her belief, she hated going to class, was not interested in doing the work and got poor grades. After some thought she was willing to ease up to an **8** on her belief for one week. Anisa decided to add the word **"maybe"** to her feelings about her teacher.

After a week she had a huge realization: "Maybe that's just how my teacher is. He's that way to everybody. It might not be about me. It doesn't bother me so much." Later, when she reported on her conviction scale it had dropped all the way to a **3**. By easing up on her conviction, she was able to see the truth. This resulted in her having a better experience and getting better grades.

A third example involves Lauren, a freshman who was bombarded with negative messages about her physical appearance. Two of her classmates repeatedly made fun of her looks. These messages eventually became strong negative beliefs on Lauren's part.

"It was easy to ignore those messages at first," she recalls. "But after awhile, I started to believe what I was hearing. I was a straight 10 on the Conviction Scale. After hearing about beliefs and their power, I decided to try to Ease Up, to take a trip down to a 6."

Lauren took action when she used the Ease Up technique by:

- removing the mirror from her school locker;
- throwing away all the teen beauty magazines that were sending her negative messages about herself;
- stopping the continual comparisons of herself to every other girl in her classes.

"Pretty soon after that," she says, "I found myself a lot happier, not only with my appearance, but with my life. I was at 6 for a couple weeks, then headed down to a 2 after that. I still have my moments of doubt, but I'm a lot more comfortable with myself these days."

EASE UP TIPS FOR FALSE BELIEFS

Easing up isn't just saying you are going to ease up. Easing up also requires doing something. The following list includes ways you can actually ease up.

Every time you have the strong belief	If you find yourself looking for evidence to prove your strong belief to be true	Identify a behavior that would be consistent with a lower level of conviction. If you think a class is extremely boring, decide to
<ul><li>say to yourself, "Not now."</li><li>say to yourself, "Maybe."</li><li>state the opposite; challenge your belief.</li></ul>	<ul><li>you ease up by looking for evidence that your conviction may not be true.</li></ul>	<ul><li>stop seeking support for your false belief by complaining.</li><li>do homework for that class every night.</li><li>give your teacher your full attention for the first ten minutes of every class.</li></ul>

TWO TENDENCIES, TWO FRAMES

It seems like most human beings have these two tendencies.

- We like people who we believe like us.
- We don't like people who we believe don't like us.

If Anisa thinks that her teacher doesn't like her, she has a tendency to not like her back. She might express this by not paying attention or not doing homework. In this way she punishes the teacher for not liking her.

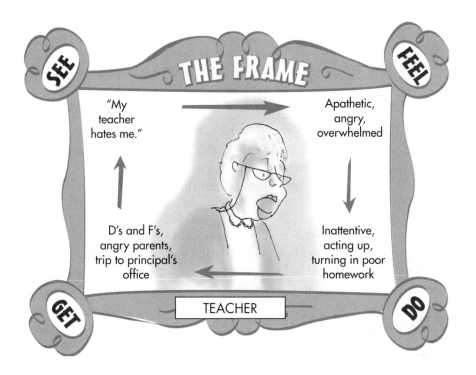

When her teacher picks up on these vibes, what will she do? Because she wants Anisa to learn, the teacher might get on her case. But to Anisa her getting on her case is further proof that she doesn't like her. Now she becomes even more irresponsible in class and nastier towards the teacher. She has created the evidence that proves that her belief is true. What really has happened? Anisa is caught in a cycle that blinds her from seeing the truth. She is stuck.

The only way for Anisa to get unstuck is to break this cycle. The way to break the cycle is to ease up on the belief. Then the whole energy changes. If she starts seeing differently, she will feel and act differently and will, therefore, get different results.

Anisa's situation can be examined through **The Frame.** Her beliefs (true or false) influence her feelings. Her feelings influence her actions and her actions influence the results she gets. These results reinforce her original belief. Her beliefs will lead to the results that will prove, in her mind, that her beliefs are true.

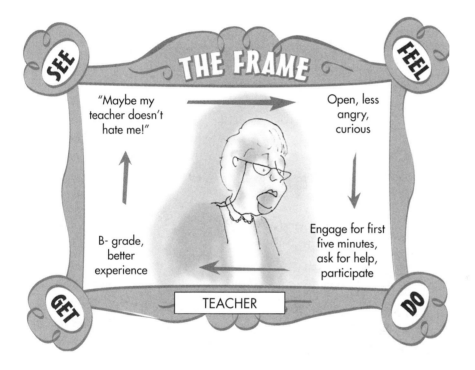

What's the downside of negative beliefs? After all, negative beliefs may be true. What if your teacher really doesn't like you? Why is holding on to that belief not in your best interest? You can't afford to hold on to that belief because it will pull out the worst in you. It will draw from you a negative energy causing the person who dislikes you to make all kinds of problems for you. But what if you reframe or think a different way about this situation?

Because they see beliefs differently, Top 20s enjoy a better quality of life and relationships. On the highway of life, they enjoy a better ride.

Top 20 Beliefs	Bottom 80 Beliefs
Know that beliefs are powerful	Are unaware of the power of beliefs
Distinguish beliefs from facts	Confuse beliefs with facts
Are willing to look at what they believe and assess whether their beliefs are true or false	Are set in their beliefs and never consider changing their beliefs as a way of improving their lives
Are willing to let go of false beliefs	Hang on to false beliefs
Are willing to ease up on their conviction	Are unwilling to ease up on their conviction
Open themselves to experiences that might change their beliefs	Avoid experiences that might change their beliefs

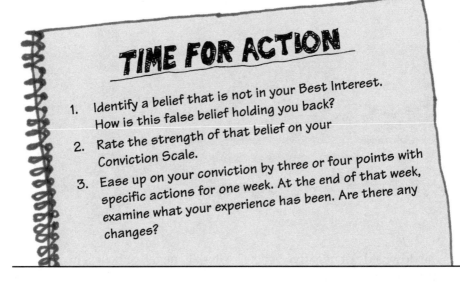

TIME FOR ACTION

1. Identify a belief that is not in your Best Interest. How is this false belief holding you back?

2. Rate the strength of that belief on your Conviction Scale.

3. Ease up on your conviction by three or four points with specific actions for one week. At the end of that week, examine what your experience has been. Are there any changes?

Above & Below The Line

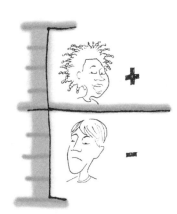

Let's imagine the working condition of a bicycle. If you knew that your bike was in perfect condition (good brakes, oiled chain, adjusted gears, air in tires), you'd be very comfortable in going on a five-mile trip to your friend's house. If the bike was not in good working condition (squeaky brakes, loose chain, no gears, low air in tires), you'd be reluctant to use it on that trek. Sometimes your bike is working in your best interest; sometimes it's not.

Our thinking works in much the same way. There are times when our thinking is working in our best interest and times when it is not. Because Top 20s are aware of their thinking, they know when it's serving them well (when to take the bike for a ride) and when it's not (when to leave the bike in the garage).

Look at the illustration of the model on the right. The vertical line is **The Ruler**. It measures the quality of our thinking: our **states of mind, attitudes, moods, or beliefs.**

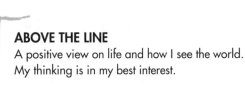

ABOVE THE LINE
A positive view on life and how I see the world. My thinking is in my best interest.

Energetic moods and emotions
• Positive attitudes • True beliefs • Hopefulness
• Optimism • Power to control my life (90/10)

BELOW THE LINE
A negative view on life and how I see the world. My thinking is _not_ in my best interest. Depressing moods and emotions
• Feelings of sadness and anger
• Negative attitudes • False beliefs • Hopelessness
• Pessimism • Powerless victim of life (10/90)

THE LINE

THE RULER

The horizontal line is simply **The Line**. This line separates The Ruler into top and bottom thinking, or **Above The Line (ATL)** or **Below The Line (BTL)**. Our attitudes, beliefs, and moods Above The Line are significantly different than Below The Line. This difference is shown in the chart above.

Sometimes students will come into our class and say, "I'm Below The Line," which indicates that they are having a bad day. When we are **BTL, our thought life is serving us poorly.** We are at the mercy of our negative attitudes and our low moods.

When we are **ATL, our thinking power is serving us well.** It is really doing the job it is designed to do whether we are aware of it or not. When we are ATL, we're really cooking. ATL thinking brings out the best in us.

All people fluctuate between these two states of mind. It's normal to have highs and lows. Top 20s sometimes experience life Below The Line. But, as you will see later, top performers handle it differently than Bottom 80s do.

Your mental and emotional experience of life is greatly influenced by your state of mind. If you are in a class and are Above The Line, you will have a totally different emotional experience than if you are Below The Line.

Teaching his sixth period class one year was a daily challenge for Tom. Going into class BTL, Tom's experience of that period was much more dreadful. Tom had a hard time trying to get the class to arrive on time, enjoy the class and do the work. However, when Tom decided to go ATL it was a better experience for both him and his students.

VIEWING PROBLEMS DIFFERENTLY

Ask yourself this question. Are you Below The Line because you have problems or do you have problems because you're Below The Line? Obviously, everyone has problems in his or her life but Top 20s and Bottom 80s view problems differently. Bottom 80s claim that they are Below The Line because they have problems in their life. Top 20s believe just the opposite. They are aware that some of the pain or misery related to their problems comes because they are perceiving life Below The Line. They also know that more effective solutions to problems are found Above The Line.

The greatest benefit of this awareness is that Top 20s know that when they are Below The Line **they still have power.** They may not be able to directly improve the condition or situation, but they can improve their attitude. They can resurface with an Above The Line attitude. What they then experience is that **the conditions of their life improve with their improved attitude.**

All people experience bad things in life but Top 20s are able to be more graceful in their suffering. Top 20s establish a resiliency regarding visits Below The Line. As they stop blaming others and take more responsibility for their lives, they visit Below The Line less often, don't stay there very long and bounce back quicker.

"It's up to you to decide: You can let sadness be your magnet or hope be your masterpiece."

–Lowen and Navarro's song
"What I Make Myself Believe"

LIFE LOOKS DIFFERENT FROM ABOVE OR BELOW THE LINE

When students are Above or Below The Line, they will see everything differently: their parents, teachers, classmates, school, homework and other activities. When parents and teachers are Above or Below The Line, they will see their children and students differently.

If you are not aware of this concept or if you forget The Line's impact on your experience, it will look like it's <u>the event</u> that is the sole source of whatever you are feeling or experiencing. Remember the outside event is only a small part (10%) of your experience but the much bigger source (90%) is your inside reality.

When you realize whether you are BTL or ATL, you are accepting responsibility to maintain the power you have to lead, direct and create your own life. Awareness cures. With awareness you can make things better; without it you can't. **It is easier to change your attitude than it is to change your outside life** (parents, teachers, school, job), but if you change your state of mind you will change the experience you have in life. Quite simply, you'll have a better ride.

> *"Usually at school I have a good morning and a bad afternoon. I wanted this to stop so I decided that in the afternoon I would think Above The Line. I tried this out and, although I didn't have the best afternoon, it was a lot better than usual."*
> – Nick

LIVING AND VISITING

It's neither good nor bad to be Above or Below The Line. It's just a life thing, a human thing. However, there's a big difference between **living** versus **visiting.** Where you think most of the time is where you live. Top 20s learn how to live Above The Line even when external conditions **aren't** favorable.

Furthermore, when Top 20s visit **Below The Line**, they

- have an awareness of being BTL.
- take responsibility for being BTL.
- develop skills to change their state of mind when they are BTL.
- don't take their BTL thinking at face value.

Consequently, **they avoid making important decisions when they are Below The Line**. It's not that they run from their problems. Rather, they do first things first. First, Top 20s get their heads on right, or get their thinking right, and then deal with the problem. In other words, they first get ATL and then make their decisions.

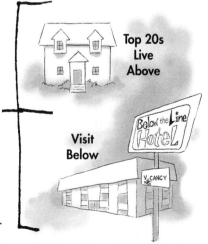

Top 20s
Live
Above

Visit
Below

Below the Line
Hotel

VACANCY

> *"My friend was kidding with me in a friendly way. She meant no harm, but I was Below The Line. I got really defensive and snapped. A little thing became really big because I made a decision to get upset when I was Below The Line."*
> —Will

MAINTAINING DIGNITY BELOW THE LINE

One thing you need to be especially careful about is being BTL without dignity or grace. It's like being underwater without oxygen. Being BTL makes you flail your arms and legs about and run the risk of emotionally hurting someone else or yourself.

In order to avoid this, think about going under water in a submarine. If you're in a submarine you'll have ample air and can put up the periscope to see where you are and what you might bump into. Being in a submarine is a metaphor for maintaining your dignity and handling your BTL visits in such a way that you protect yourself and others from harm.

One day Tom, as a classroom teacher, learned about being Below The Line without dignity the hard way. Upset about students not having their homework done or misbehaving, Tom foolishly overreacted. He once suspended a student only to be told when he went to the principal's office that he didn't have the authority to suspend a student. Now when Tom goes BTL, he tries to go in the submarine and maintain his dignity. If this happens in class, he will even make a submarine diving sound to inform his students that he's going under. Now his visits BTL are fewer, shorter and much more graceful. Consequently, he has fewer messes to clean up afterwards.

INDICATORS, TRIGGERS AND TRAMPOLINES

What's life like for you Below The Line? Those BTL feelings and reactions are your **indicators**. Some of these include the following.

- **Feelings:** anger, frustration, sadness, inadequacy, jealousy, depression
- **Reactions:** withdrawing, yelling, judging, fighting, arguing

Do you know what your indicators are when you are BTL?

Everybody behaves differently when they are BTL. When Mary is BTL she feels overwhelmed that no one is helping her. She feels unloved and becomes teary-eyed. When Tom is BTL he talks faster and gets louder. Michael's indicator is that he begins to see people in his life doing things wrong. Paul's indicator of being BTL is manifested in his desire to take control of the situation. Willow withdraws, worries and dwells on negative thoughts. The BTL experience is different for everyone.

The other important thing to be aware of is what **triggers** us to go Below. **Triggers are those conditions that make it likely for us to go BTL.** Maybe it's

- somebody calling you stupid or laughing at something you say.
- not finding a seat at the lunch table with the crowd you want to be with.
- doing poorly on a test or assignment.
- a parent telling you to do something or that you can't do something you want to do.
- being sick or in pain.

Maybe you just woke up BTL. Knowing your triggers and your indicators can help you be more resilient in bouncing from below to above.

Remember that **one choice you always have is to wait until you are better able to decide** what the best action would be. It is always a good choice not to say or do something that you would later regret or something that would send you even further Below The Line. Remember the broken bicycle? It may be wise to not make any decisions until your thinking has been repaired and you have surfaced Above The Line.

Just as you have a trigger that tends to get you moving BTL, you can create your own positive triggers. Examples of ATL triggers include the following helpful hints.

- Spending some quiet time alone
  - Talking to a trusted friend or adult
  - Listening to music
  - Exercising
  - Performing an act of service for someone who needs help
  - Praying or meditating
  - Focusing on the present
  - Waiting until tomorrow

"I constantly tell myself to be happy. When I wake up in the morning I <u>decide</u> I am going to have a good day, and I usually do."

– Angie

These are all things that might help get your perspective back and get your head screwed on right. See these perspective-changing ideas as **trampolines** since they help us to bounce back up Above The Line.

If you find yourself bogged down in a Below The Line experience, the fastest way to get unstuck is to stop thinking of whatever is putting you BTL. The simplest way to do this is to focus on the present. Focus on whatever is in front of you now. If you are having a BTL experience and your next class is history, see your history class as a means of getting your mind away from what is keeping you below. Use the history class as an opportunity to concentrate on something else.

ALERT AND PROTECT OTHERS

Top 20s do something else when they are BTL. They communicate that they are BTL to other people so others understand that they are not the source of the problem. Sometimes just telling someone you're Below helps you to move upward.

When Paul met with Mary to work on this book, she informed him of having a bad day. Mary smashed her toe earlier and the pain triggered her to go Below The Line. Aware of her negative attitude and, by informing Paul up front, Mary's mood didn't diminish the productivity of their meeting. Had she been unaware of being BTL or had not communicated it to Paul, he might have taken her bad mood personally. Their energy for the meeting would have gone in a totally different direction. However, because she alerted Paul that she was BTL, he knew the cause of her emotional state. Consequently, their meeting was quite productive and no damage was done to their relationship.

"I see my family at the hardest times of the day when I'm Below The Line. I see them in the morning when I am usually very tired and after school when I'm exhausted from the day. When they try to talk to me about my attitude, I find anything to blame it on. I'd never take the responsibility for my unhappiness. My outlook on life was terrible. By becoming aware of being BTL, I decided I need to use a submarine when I'm angry and just separate from the group for awhile and cool down. I need to realize it's only me holding me back from being happy. I can't change anything but myself."

— Emmy

THE POWER OF MAKING IT BETTER

As we introduce you to other ideas in the book and as your understanding of this material deepens, you will more quickly detect when you are BTL and more quickly get ATL. As you accept greater responsibility for your life, you will be more aware of the power you have to steer your life, regardless of the circumstances, in the direction you want to go.

This great power of accepting responsibility will enable you to discard the weights (thoughts and beliefs which lead to non-productive behavior) that in the past have sunk you deeper Below The Line and kept you there. When you plant the powerful seeds of responsibility, you bear the wonderful fruit of freedom, a freedom that allows you to direct your own life and influence the lives of others towards having a good ride.

Let's look at it this way. You are only given a certain number of days to spend on this planet. When all is said and done, you want to accumulate as many "good" days as possible. Awareness of the Line gives you the power to choose just how your days are going to be spent. You have the power to limit "bad hair days" or "sad Monday mornings" from popping up on your calendar.

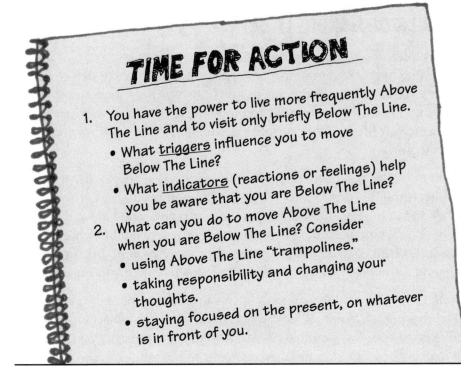

TIME FOR ACTION

1. You have the power to live more frequently Above The Line and to visit only briefly Below The Line.
   - What <u>triggers</u> influence you to move Below The Line?
   - What <u>indicators</u> (reactions or feelings) help you be aware that you are Below The Line?

2. What can you do to move Above The Line when you are Below The Line? Consider
   - using Above The Line "trampolines."
   - taking responsibility and changing your thoughts.
   - staying focused on the present, on whatever is in front of you.

Eliminating Thought Circles

Thought Circles are mental habits that are likely to occur when people are Below The Line. When someone is experiencing Thought Circles one thought leads to another and another and another like a snowball getting larger and larger as it rolls down a hill. Each individual thought may or may not be logically connected to the previous thought. Thought Circles spiral in a rapid descent until you are far Below The Line.

After soccer practice Trent is waiting for a ride home from his parents.

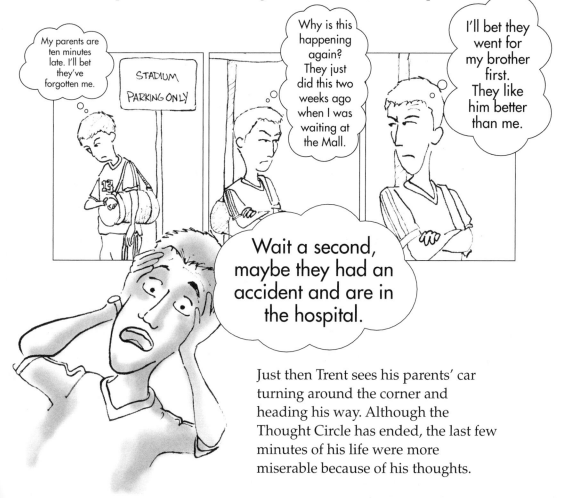

My parents are ten minutes late. I'll bet they've forgotten me.

STADIUM
PARKING ONLY

Why is this happening again? They just did this two weeks ago when I was waiting at the Mall.

I'll bet they went for my brother first. They like him better than me.

Wait a second, maybe they had an accident and are in the hospital.

Just then Trent sees his parents' car turning around the corner and heading his way. Although the Thought Circle has ended, the last few minutes of his life were more miserable because of his thoughts.

THE WORRY THOUGHT CIRCLE

What we are talking about here is the anatomy of worry. Trent's Thought Circle formed because he allowed his thoughts to

- jump to conclusions.
- imagine the worst possible outcome.
- be highly judgmental.

You can see from Trent's situation how Thought Circles send us deeper and deeper Below The Line. As we get deeper Below The Line, it is more difficult to stop the circle from expanding even further. The sooner we realize we are having a Thought Circle the easier it is to stop it.

It would have been in Trent's Best Interest to handle this differently. "Darn, my parents are ten minutes late. I'll bet they've forgotten me. Oops...this looks like the beginning of a Thought Circle. I better stick with the facts. All I know is that they are ten minutes late."

Sometimes we observe Thought Circles forming in the minds of our students. This can happen when a student gets a note in class to report to the office…

"My mom found a lump on her arm and immediately thought it was cancer. She said, 'If I die who's going to take care of the family? I'm not gonna be able to go on the trip this summer.' I turned to her, 'Mom, relax. You haven't even had it tested yet. You're just gonna keep making yourself even more miserable.'"

– Maria

I'll bet school found out about the party Saturday night.

I wonder who turned us in.

I'll bet it was Joe. I saw him leave math class early and go to the office.

I'm going to get suspended. My parents are going to really be mad.

I'll be grounded for the rest of my life. And I'll never be able to drive the car again. I'm dead!

These are times when we tell our students, "Don't let your Thought Circle become the problem." In other words, don't let your thinking make the original problem worse than it already is. **Let the problem be the problem** by understanding the original problem and only dealing with that. Otherwise, your ever-widening Thought Circle will send you spiraling deep Below The Line.

THE ANGRY THOUGHT CIRCLE

Remember, it doesn't take long for a Thought Circle to go from a first thought to the tenth thought. This happens in just a few seconds. It doesn't take long to work yourself into a frenzy and create a real mess for yourself and others.

Imagine that Cecilia is watching TV downstairs when she hears her mother call from upstairs…

What you've just seen is the anatomy of anger. In just one minute this angry thought circle cost Cecilia the opportunity to

- have a great time shopping with her mom at the mall.

- enjoy watching her movie.

- have her mother want to do something special for Cecilia in the future.

- take responsibility for her actions because she blamed her mother for this mess.

ANGER

These opportunities are lost not because someone was trying to make Cecilia's life miserable but because of her angry Thought Circle. If you want to experience something better and act in your Best Interest, you first need to change negative thinking and stop Thought Circles in their tracks. You have this power. Use it.

STOP THOUGHT CIRCLES IN THEIR TRACKS

One simple way to stop Thought Circles is to use the "Not Now" technique. Whenever you catch yourself beginning a Thought Circle, say: "Stop. This is a Thought Circle. Not Now."

Sometimes the concern that is the origin of a Thought Circle does need to be seriously considered. When you are unable to give a problem or situation the attention it may require at the time, put that issue in your mental **Parking Lot** until later. Make an appointment with yourself to deal with it after school. Then focus on whatever is in front of you. Stay in the present. Because you will not have spent the whole day Below The Line, you will probably approach the situation after school by being closer to or Above The Line. Consequently, you will make a better decision or have a better experience.

Using "Not Now" or deciding to put things in the mental **Parking Lot** are ways of taking control of your life rather than being controlled. They are ways of creating a good ride for yourself by dealing with concerns when you are best able to do so.

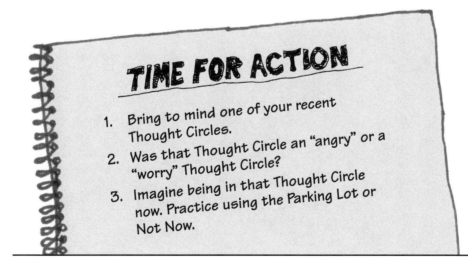

TIME FOR ACTION

1. Bring to mind one of your recent Thought Circles.

2. Was that Thought Circle an "angry" or a "worry" Thought Circle?

3. Imagine being in that Thought Circle now. Practice using the Parking Lot or Not Now.

The Influence of Messages

Throughout history courageous men and women have risked their lives for the sake of discovery. The desire to discover, explore and know is wired into the core of who we are as human beings. But what about you? What is the most important discovery that you could make?

The most important discovery that you can make in your life
is to discover **WHO YOU ARE.**

The most important people in your life are those people
who help you discover **WHO YOU ARE.**

The most important thing you can do for other people
is to help them discover **WHO THEY ARE.**

This is a pretty serious chapter because it has to do with this very important discovery: who you truly are, who you think you are, and how you come to know who you are.

THE POWER OF THE SOCIAL MIRROR

How do you come to know who you are? Obviously, there are countless ways you come to know who you are. These include family and relatives, friends and classmates, involvement in school or church, participation in extracurriculars or organizations, life experiences, the media, and so on. These are all a part of your **social mirror** which reflects back to you an image of who you are. The primary way these reflections come to you is through **messages.** In other words, an important way you come to know who you are is by verbal and non-verbal messages that come from others.

YOU ARE A MESSAGE CENTER

Think of yourself as a message center. Thousands of messages bombard you each day. Some messages are important; some are trivial. The most important messages are those dealing with who others think you are or want you to be. Some of these messages are obvious; some are not.

As a message center you need to understand some very important things about messages. The most important thing is **the power of messages.** Messages have influence. They influence what you think about and how you think.

THE VALIDITY AND INTERPRETATION OF MESSAGES

Another important consideration regarding messages is their validity. Is the message true or false? Each message that comes to you is also interpreted by you. You interpret each message as being either true or false. The validity of the message and your interpretation of the message creates four possibilities.

FOUR MESSAGE POSSIBILITIES	
1	If you receive a **FALSE** message but interpret it as **TRUE**, you are now believing what is **FALSE.**
2	If you receive a **TRUE** message and interpret it as **FALSE**, you are now believing what is **FALSE.**
3	If you receive a **TRUE** message and interpret it as **TRUE**, you are now believing what is **TRUE.**
4	If you receive a **FALSE** message but interpret it as **FALSE**, you are now believing what is **TRUE**.

THE QUALITY OF YOUR LIFE

Because you are a message center the quality of your life and relationships will be greatly influenced by how well you interpret the validity of messages. Top 20s are very good at interpreting true messages as true and false messages as false. If you are able to do that the quality of your life will improve. Bottom 80s will more often interpret true messages as false and false messages as true. If you fall into this category, the quality of your life and relationships will decline.

The reason for this is that messages **in-form**. Once a message gets **in** you, it tends to **form** you. It forms the way you see yourself. It forms your opinions and attitudes. It forms your beliefs. If all of these important things are being formed by what is false, they will have a negative impact on your life. If they are being formed by what is true, they will have a positive impact on your life.

The following story offers some good examples of this.

Parable of the Eagle

A certain man went through a forest seeking any bird of interest he might find. He caught a young eagle, brought it home, and put it among his fowls and ducks and turkeys, and gave it chickens' food to eat even though it was an eagle, the king of birds.

Five years later a naturalist came to see him and, after passing through his garden, said, "That bird is an eagle, not a chicken."

"Yes," said its owner, "but I have trained it to be a chicken. It is no longer an eagle. It is a chicken even though it measures eight feet from tip to tip of its wings."

"No," said the naturalist, "it is an eagle still; it has the heart of an eagle, and I will make it soar high up to the heavens."

"No," said the owner, "it is a chicken and it will never fly."

They agreed to test it. The naturalist picked up the eagle, held it up, and said with great intensity, "Eagle, you are an eagle; you belong to the sky and not to this earth; stretch forth your wings and fly."

The eagle turned this way and that, and then, looking down, saw the chickens eating their food, and down he jumped.

The owner said, "I told you it was a chicken."

"No," said the naturalist, "it is an eagle. Give it another chance tomorrow."

So the next day he took it to the top of the house and said, "Eagle, you are an eagle; stretch forth your wings and fly." But again the eagle, seeing the chickens feeding, jumped down and fed with them.

Then the owner said, "I told you it was a chicken."

"No," asserted the naturalist, "it is an eagle, and it still has the heart of an eagle; only give it one more chance, and I will make it fly tomorrow."

The next morning he rose early and took the eagle outside the city, away from the houses, to the foot of a high mountain. The sun was just rising, gilding the top of the mountain with gold, and every crag was glistening in the joy of that beautiful morning.

He picked up the eagle and said to it, "Eagle, you are an eagle; you belong to the sky and not to this earth; stretch forth your wings and fly!"

The eagle looked around and trembled as if new life were coming to it. But it did not fly. The naturalist then made it look straight at the sun. Suddenly, it stretched out its wings and, with the screech of an eagle, it mounted higher and higher and never returned. It was an eagle, though it had been kept and tamed as a chicken!

BECOMING AN EAGLE

The messages sent to the eagle in this story have a powerful influence. More powerful than the messages, however, is the eagle's own interpretation of the messages' validity. The eagle's interpretation of the messages it receives becomes its beliefs. The same is true for you. The messages you interpret as true become your beliefs.

INTERPRETING MESSAGES	
1	If you receive a **FALSE** message (You are a chicken.), but interpret it as **TRUE** (I am a chicken.), you are now believing what is **FALSE**.
2	If you receive a **TRUE** message (You are an eagle.), and interpret it as **FALSE** (I am a chicken.), you are now believing what is **FALSE**.
3	If you receive a **TRUE** message (You are an eagle.), and interpret it as **TRUE** (I am an eagle.), you are now believing what is **TRUE**.
4	If you receive a **FALSE** message (You are a chicken.), but interpret it as **FALSE** (I am an eagle.), you are now believing what is **TRUE**.

Let's see how this happens for the eagle:

The eagle's full potential and the quality of its life are **influenced** by the messages it receives but **determined** by the eagle's own beliefs about those messages. If the farmer sent the message that the eagle was a chicken but the eagle responded, "Wrong. You're mistaken. I'm an eagle," then the farmer's message would have no power over the eagle.

Messages that you allow to become beliefs have a powerful influence in your own life. True messages that become your beliefs will help you develop your potential. False messages that become your beliefs will block your potential.

THE BURNING MATCH

Imagine someone telling you to hold on to a burning match. You are told not to drop it or blow it out. As the flame gets closer to your fingers, you realize you're about to get burned. Now what? Do you continue to hold on to the match or do you blow it out or drop it even though you were told not to?

Messages can be like a burning match. False messages can "burn" or hurt you if you hold on to them long enough. These dangerous messages need to be dropped.

Clark is a very talented and highly successful 40-year old man. He is respected by his colleagues for his honesty, kindness, and contributions he makes to the company. People like working and socializing with Clark. But Clark is unhappy and never finds satisfaction in his work or relationships. He feels inadequate. Why is that? False messages.

As a high school student Clark worked as a carpenter with his father. No matter how hard Clark tried, his father constantly criticized his work. The board was never cut right or nailed straight enough to satisfy his father. Even if someone else was responsible for the work his father was unhappy with, Clark would often be the one who was blamed. Usually the father's criticism came when other workers were present.

Can you see the burning match that Clark has hung on to for over 25 years? Do you see how his father sent him a false message that Clark accepted as true? Do you see how Clark's interpretation of this message, "I am inadequate. I never do anything right," has negatively influenced his life?

"I am so glad you taught us this metaphor. I am going to use it on the girl who has been cruel to me. When she says something cruel to me, I will just say to myself, 'Just let it go.' I can't let her get to me."
– Bri

Now what? Can Clark let go of the harmful false message that is spoiling his life? Can he change his interpretation of this false message and see it as false? If he can, he will become the eagle he truly is.

Again, Top 20s are very adept at recognizing and hanging on to true messages and spotting and letting go of false messages. That's why Top 20s are able to soar.

INFLUENCE: THE POWER OF TEEN CULTURE

Influence is a subtle but awesome power that changes the action or thinking of another person. Sometimes the influence is direct and intentional; sometimes it's indirect and unplanned. Sometimes it's in your Best Interest and sometimes it's in your Worst Interest. To some extent it is probably true that everyone is influenced and everyone influences.

A major influence on all people is the culture in which they live. Adolescents are influenced strongly by their own Teen Culture. Top 20 teens are very aware of the power of peer and media influence. In particular, they are aware of the negative influence Teen Culture can have on youth. Top 20 teens know the influence of peers and media is not always in their Best Interest and can, in fact, have a negative impact on their health, relationships and self-image.

Top 20 teens are aware of the following questions regarding Teen Culture influences.

- What do they have me wearing, eating or drinking?
- What do they have me doing or saying?
- What do they have me thinking or feeling?
- Where do they have me going?
- What do they have me becoming?

"Your 'coolness' is judged very early by your friends, by the dolls or trucks you have, or even if you have 64 or 96 colors in your crayon box. Later, it becomes clothes or cell phones. It starts with the media but it comes down to the people we see every day, our peers."

— Kayla

PEER INFLUENCE

Think back to being in a group in grade school. Can you recall something that became a value of that group? Something you needed to have? A way you needed to act or a commonly-used phrase?

What you remember is probably the result of group influence. Although you may not have been aware of this influence at the time, it was present and active. Perhaps the other group members weren't even aware of their influence on you. Nonetheless, influence was taking place.

Some influence will nudge us in one direction and some influence will nudge us in another direction. Top 20s have a sharp awareness of when there is influence on them and the direction in which that influence is pushing. They also know that they are not completely controlled by peer influence. They still are free and responsible for making their own decisions.

MEDIA INFLUENCE

"When we shop at the mall, all we see are the models with their perfect bodies. When we're there we laugh about how skinny they are, but when we get home, we complain about how fat we are. The media is wearing away our self-esteem."
— Emily

Today the powerful unseen force of media influence has become stronger than ever. As families have been forced to produce double incomes, many kids are being "raised" by the media. Teens are bombarded by the overwhelming influence from television, radio, magazines, video games and the internet. Young people get over 3,000 marketing images per day through their media contacts.

It's big business. American teens spend over $100 billion annually; their parents spend another $50 billion on them. Kids want what's "cool" and the media determines just what that will be.

Whereas Bottom 80 teens are overly influenced by peers and media, Top 20 teens are able to filter Teen Culture messages through The Truth. Able to distinguish between messages that are true and messages that are false, teens are less likely to be influenced in ways that are contrary to their Best Interest. They are not likely to be influenced in ways contrary to their true selves, good health, and positive relationships.

You have the power and responsibility to decide whether the messages that come from The Truth or the messages from Teen Culture will influence you. Which of these messages is a shining light that can help you discover the path to a joyful and satisfying life? Which message is a burning match that will damage your life and relationships?

Those things which are most meaningful to you as a person are impossible if you believe the popular message of the Teen Culture. Let's take friendship as an example. True friendship is impossible if you accept the Teen Culture message as true. You will need to pretend to be someone you're not.

Your friends will never really know you and, if your friends are also pretending, you will never know them. True friendship requires that you are real with each other and being real only happens if you can accept yourself.

Doesn't the message of The Truth actually describe what friendship is? Don't true friends find each other to be wonderful and feel a sense of belonging and acceptance of each other. Doesn't a true friend help you be your true and real self while encouraging you to be on the outside who you are on the inside?

Hang on to messages that give life and let go of messages that are harmful. You are the interpreter of true and false messages and your interpretation will make **the big difference**.

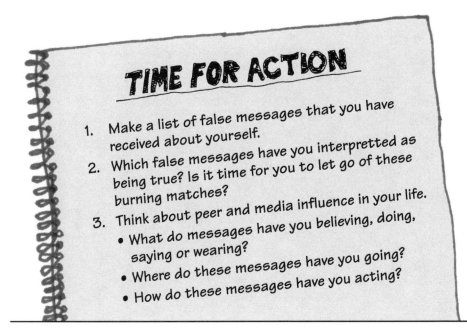

TIME FOR ACTION

1. Make a list of false messages that you have received about yourself.

2. Which false messages have you interpretted as being true? Is it time for you to let go of these burning matches?

3. Think about peer and media influence in your life.
   • What do messages have you believing, doing, saying or wearing?
   • Where do these messages have you going?
   • How do these messages have you acting?

Learning from Our Mistakes

One thing Top 20s and Bottom 80s have in common is that they are mistake makers. In fact, because they tend to be risk takers, Top 20s probably make more mistakes than Bottom 80s. But the significant difference between the two, as you might expect by now, is the way Top 20s respond to the mistakes they make.

OTHERS RESPOND TO OUR MISTAKES

Whether we are a Top 20 or a Bottom 80, the way we think, learn and communicate about mistakes is influenced by how others have responded to us when we have made one. As you will see, the response that others make to us when we make a mistake is one of the most powerful experiences we will have.

There is a wide range of responses people have when we make a mistake.

Although there is a wide range of possible responses to our mistakes, usually the responses are quite negative. Often after mistakes people

- criticize.
- don't trust us anymore.
- ignore us.
- talk behind our backs.
- are disappointed.
- turn against us.

- are irate, mad, or angry.
- yell and punish.
- judge.
- give dirty looks.
- freak out.
- are sarcastic.

If these are the responses we get when we make a mistake, the message is loud and clear, "YOU BETTER NOT MAKE A MISTAKE."

THE FLASHLIGHT STORY

Although not an electrician, Michael Cole's father tried to repair wiring in his own home and for relatives. Since the electricity to the house had to be turned off while his father worked on the wiring, young Michael's job was to hold the flashlight so his father could see. If his father couldn't get something to work, he would always rage and swear at Michael for how he was holding the flashlight, "Michael, you're good for nothing. You never do anything right." If his father became displeased a second time, the punishment would become even more severe.

Michael learned three powerful lessons from this experience.

1. He couldn't do anything right. Nothing short of perfection was acceptable.

2. He learned to fear and deny mistakes. At first he would lie. If that didn't work, he would blame someone else.

3. He believed that the lesson in any mistake came only through the punishment. As an adult when his father was no longer present, Michael would dwell on his mistakes and punish himself.

It wasn't until the age of 48 when Michael heard the following popcorn story that he realized there was a better response to mistakes. He could learn from the mistake without requiring punishment. He could keep the lesson and throw away the mistake.

THE POPCORN STORY

One night seven-year old Paul Bernabei wanted to make popcorn. While his parents were in the living room, he undertook his cooking adventure in the kitchen. He put oil into a pot and placed it on the hot burner. Once the oil was hot, Paul reached up to pour popcorn seeds into the pot. Unfortunately, when the plastic bag containing the seeds touched the hot pot, a hole melted in the bag and popcorn seeds spilled all over the stove, counter and floor.

Upon hearing this commotion, Paul's parents rushed into the kitchen and immediately asked, "Are you OK?"

"Yes," Paul answered. Although startled by what had happened, he had not been burned.

"Are you sure?"

"Yes, I'm fine," Paul replied.

"Good," said his parents, "we'll help you clean up the mess."

Paul and his parents spent the next ten minutes on the floor picking up the seeds.

Paul's popcorn mistake and the way his parents responded to him made a powerful mental and emotional imprint on him and resulted in his learning three important lessons.

1. Paul was more important than a mistake. Because his parents' immediate concern was for his well-being and not for the popcorn mess, Paul experienced deep value and worth. Certainly this was reinforced by his parents many times throughout his life.

2. Be there when people mess up. One of our purposes in life is to help others when they experience difficulties. It is not our responsibility to "clean it up" for them, but to support them in making things better.

3. Mistakes are wonderful. Because many wonderful things can be learned from mistakes and risk-taking, they are to be valued, not avoided.

This experience taught Paul the attitude and belief that mistakes are beneficial. **In fact, it is the belief that mistakes are beneficial that makes mistakes beneficial for Top 20s.** It is the belief that mistakes are to be avoided that results in mistakes not being beneficial for Bottom 80s.

Paul's parents responded to him when he made the popcorn mistake by affirming him and his worth. As wonderful as that response is, it probably isn't common. How others respond to us after a mistake will influence how we respond to future mistakes.

OUR RESPONSE TO MISTAKES

Whether we are aware of it or not, we respond to every mistake we make. These responses fall into four categories.

1. We **deny** a mistake by verbally or mentally stating, "It didn't happen." We don't talk about it. We block it out of our mind. If someone else brings it up, we deny it or get defensive.

2. We acknowledge the mistake but **blame** someone else for it. This may take the form of "He did it" or "She made me do it." We blame in order to get off the hook. In blaming others we avoid responsibility.

3. We **justify** the mistake. We make excuses or offer "good" reasons for making the mistake. We may explain to a teacher, "I couldn't get my homework done last night because my family was celebrating my grandmother's birthday" or "My soccer game went into overtime so I couldn't study for the test."

4. We **dwell** on it by focusing on nothing else but the mistake. We allow the mistake to overwhelm us. We allow the mistake to define us: "I'm so stupid. I never do anything right. I'll never be able to get over this."

5. We **own** it by looking the mistake squarely in the eye. We take responsibility and **learn** the lesson life is trying to teach us. We use the mistake as a teacher: "I just made a mistake. What can I learn from this?"

When we operate like a Bottom 80 and respond to mistakes by denying, blaming, justifying or dwelling, we are likely to repeat the mistake over and over again. Life will offer us many opportunities to learn. By being a Top 20 who owns and learns from mistakes, we are not likely to repeat them. Since the purpose of mistakes is to learn a lesson, once the lesson is learned there is no further need to focus on the mistake.

Paul once served on the administrative team of a high school. The head school administrator sometimes said at a team meeting, "I made a decision that was a mistake. I want to talk about this and have you help me understand what happened so I'll learn from this and do it better next time."

That's the attitude of a Top 20 and the attitude of a leader most of us would be very willing to follow.

GETTING TO THE BIG LEARNING

This chapter on mistakes is closely connected to the next chapter on Comfort Zone and risk-taking. Because it's easy for us to do things that are **inside** our Comfort Zone, we may not want to try things that are **outside** our Comfort Zone.

But where's the Big Learning in life? Isn't it outside our Comfort Zone? In order to get the Big Learning, we're probably going to make some mistakes. Thomas Edison failed a thousand times before he discovered a workable filament for the light bulb. Like Edison, we need to go through mistakes if we're ever going to get Big Learning.

But if we're afraid to make mistakes, we'll hang out in the safety of our Comfort Zone. Sheryl was a pretty good basketball player in junior high school. She was an outstanding right-handed dribbler who could often get past her defender to the basket. Her coach encouraged her to practice dribbling left-handed. Because Sheryl was uncomfortable dribbling left-handed and often made

mistakes, she refused to practice her left-handed dribble. Once she got to high school, her opponents realized she couldn't dribble left-handed. When they stopped her from dribbling to her right, Sheryl's success on the court dropped tremendously.

Taking risks and learning from mistakes is a habit of Top 20s. The more we do it, the more we learn and the easier it becomes. Learning from mistakes enables Top 20s to succeed at a higher level. It prevents us from getting stuck along the road and provides us with a better ride.

> *"Failure is the opportunity to begin again more intelligently."*
> – Henry Ford

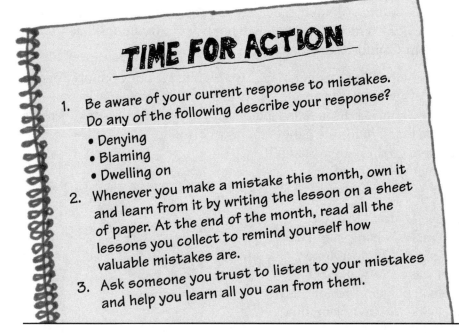

TIME FOR ACTION

1. Be aware of your current response to mistakes. Do any of the following describe your response?

   • Denying
   • Blaming
   • Dwelling on

2. Whenever you make a mistake this month, own it and learn from it by writing the lesson on a sheet of paper. At the end of the month, read all the lessons you collect to remind yourself how valuable mistakes are.

3. Ask someone you trust to listen to your mistakes and help you learn all you can from them.

Growing through Risk

Comfort Zone is an important concept for both Top 20s and Bottom 80s. Inside our Comfort Zone we feel comfortable and safe. Everything is known, predictable and within our control. The further we go outside our Comfort Zone the more we feel uncomfortable and unsafe. Everything seems unknown, unpredictable and beyond our control.

Your Comfort Zone is a very important place for you. You need a place to feel safe where you have control over your life. Although it is one of the most necessary parts of your life, **your Comfort Zone can also destroy you.**

"Dude, so my Comfort Zone is important, but it can, like, destroy me? Isn't that a contradiction?"

"A Comfort Zone is like being caught in quicksand. It's soft and warm and squishy between your toes. But unless you get out, it will eventually suffocate you."
– Will

It's actually a paradox, a statement seemingly contradictory and absurd that may actually be true. Comfort Zone is a necessary place but it can interfere with your growth and well-being. If your Comfort Zone is to exist for your growth and benefit, and not your destruction, then it needs to be **a place that you go from and a place to which you return.** Your Comfort Zone becomes destructive when it's a place where you permanently stay.

OUR NEED FOR SECURITY AND CHALLENGE

Life requires two things: security and challenge. Security is provided inside the Comfort Zone and challenge is provided outside it. As human beings we need both security and challenges. One without the other would limit our growth.

Anytime we're outside our Comfort Zone, we may hate how we feel (anxious, uncomfortable) but love what we learn. Inside our Comfort Zone, we may love how we feel but hate that we don't learn anything new.

Top 20s understand this need for living both inside and outside their Comfort Zone. In doing so they learn how to expand it. In desiring to become more than they are, they routinely leave their Comfort Zone. Bottom 80s think the best place to be is inside their Comfort Zone. If they stay there exclusively, their Comfort Zone actually shrinks. They never become anything more than they already are.

What are some of the things inside and outside your Comfort Zone?

Here are some possibilities:

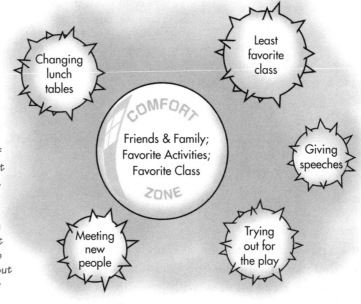

"I used to be so afraid of giving a speech. I can dance in front of 5,000 people but can't speak in front of two. When I had to give a speech, I calmed myself down, took a deep breath and got through it. I was so proud and happy about jumping out of my Comfort Zone."
– Dana

What's inside someone's Comfort Zone can be way outside someone else's. Basketball, writing papers and talking to adults are inside Georgia's Comfort Zone but they are way outside Miguel's.

STAR QUALITIES ARE FOUND OUTSIDE OUR COMFORT ZONE

Many of the things you really desire are outside your Comfort Zone. For example, the big opportunities for Star Qualities such as courage and confidence are found outside your Comfort Zone. While operating outside your Comfort Zone, you're growing as a person and a student. You're becoming. You're developing your potential. You're expanding your Comfort Zone and overcoming fear.

Here are a few common out of Comfort Zone activities that lead to success for Top 20 high school students:

"I may be outgoing around my friends, but when it comes down to meeting new people for the first time, I clam up. The Comfort Zone class in TLC made me want to change and show people who I really am."
– Karina

"I do things to grow now just because I'm not comfortable with them. I doubt I would have joined the ski team without taking TLC."
– Liz

"If you stay inside your Comfort Zone, you will never make the winning basket. If you go outside the Zone, you might."
– Jimmy

RATIONAL RISK AND IRRATIONAL FEAR

How many of the activities on the previous page are not in your Best
Interest? They are all in your Best Interest. We define Best Interest as that
which has a true and lasting benefit for you. So why don't you readily go
after these? Because every venture outside the Comfort Zone is a risk and
with every risk comes an accompanying fear. The following are some of
the most common fears:

One or more of these fears are attached to every activity outside your
Comfort Zone.

EXAMPLE

Leo is afraid of doing poorly on his math test next week.
In fact, he's afraid he might even fail the class.
Nonetheless, he's reluctant to raise his hand in math
class and has never been willing to see his teacher after
class for help. Leo fears his classmates' and teacher's
opinions. He decides to do it all by himself even though
he seems to be falling further behind because he's not
understanding the material.

What's likely to happen is that Leo will obey his fears and that his fears will then be realized. If he doesn't get help he will fail the test and eventually fail the class. His teacher will have a negative opinion about Leo that he doesn't care about math and doesn't work very hard. Furthermore, Leo will be embarrassed if he fails the class. In other words, when we succeed at being fearful, we win the prize that comes with fear.

Fear comes in two different forms. The fear of facing an uncaged lion is rational and reasonable. It is grounded in reality and our Best Interest. Leo's fear of raising his hand is irrational. Serving this fear is not in Leo's Best Interest.

Leo's other option is to push himself through his fear by raising his hand in class and seeing his teacher for help. If so, he's likely to do better on the test. He will indicate to his teacher that he's concerned about the class, wants to do well and avoid further embarrassment. But even more important, Leo has developed a bit more of one of the most important Star Qualities: courage. And having developed a bit more courage, Leo will be able to push through more fears that he will encounter in his future.

EXAMPLE

Two years later, Leo begins to struggle with his senior math class. Immediately he raises his hand and asks a question. If that doesn't clear up his confusion, he gets help from a classmate or makes an appointment to see his teacher after school. He might see his former teacher in the hall and say, "I'm struggling with math. Can you give me five minutes." His teacher comments,

"Leo, I love your attitude. Come on in."

What a difference it makes when we don't allow fear to determine the quality of our ride. Leo's Comfort Zone has expanded enormously. He has taken a giant step towards becoming a Top 20.

THE FEAR OF OPOs

Another big fear that keeps us in our Comfort Zone is OPOs—Other People's Opinions. It's always important to be open to feedback from other people because it can help us see what we need to see. When their feedback is not in our Best Interest or limits us in some way, then we need to take a different approach.

"I thought TLC was a great class until someone told me he thought it was getting old. I started to think TLC was getting dumb just because someone else did. Then I realized that was an OPO and that I had changed my whole belief on this class just because one person told me it was old. I really need to work on minimizing the importance of OPOs in my life."
– Bill

Other people's opinions of you are none of your business.

If you can accept that, much of your fear will disappear. Your opinion of you is your business. Other People's Opinions of you are their business. Most young people are jailed in their Comfort Zone because OPOs lock kids up and throw away the key.

**Freedom comes only when you believe that
Other People's Opinions are none of your business.**

"My mom has Multiple Sclerosis. She has trouble walking and uses a cane. Before TLC I would be a little embarrassed going out with her because people would stare. Now I realize that I shouldn't care about what anyone else thinks."
— Kelly

Bottom 80s think Other People's Opinions are so important they are willing to let them determine their decisions and actions. Top 20s care about Other People's Opinions but stay detached. They are not trapped in their Comfort Zone because of them. Their friends don't take a vote before Top 20s decide what to do.

You move outside your Comfort Zone so you can expand it, so you can become comfortable with things that are uncomfortable. Bottom 80s find it easier to organize their lives in such a way that they never leave their Comfort Zone. Top 20s step out of their Comfort Zone frequently and are rewarded with new experiences that expand the diameter of their sphere (see next page).

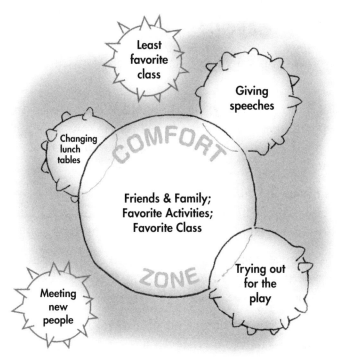

Least
favorite
class

Giving
speeches

Changing
lunch
tables

COMFORT

Friends & Family;
Favorite Activities;
Favorite Class

ZONE

Trying out
for the
play

Meeting
new
people

*"It shouldn't matter
what other people think
of your decisions. In
twenty years will it really
matter if the most
popular boy thought you
were stupid for trying
out for basketball? Make
every choice for yourself
if it makes you a
better person."*
– Claire

RECKLESS RISK-TAKING

In the first part of this chapter, we have seen that one decision that
distinguishes Top 20s from Bottom 80s is risk-taking. Top 20s are masters
at taking risks.

They also understand the difference between healthy risk-taking and
reckless risk-taking. Healthy risk-taking is taking risks that cause you to
grow (like trying out for the speech team). Reckless risk-taking inhibits
your growth and requires you to be phony, pretend or be your false self
(like doing drugs).

REASONS FOR RECKLESS RISK

Reckless risk is prevalent in Teen Culture largely due to five dominant reasons.

1. **Belief in invulnerability:** Teens often don't believe anything bad will happen to them as a result of their risk-taking: "It's not going to happen to me. If it does, it won't happen until I'm 60. Then it won't matter."

2. **Fear of missing out:** Teens fear missing out what the group is experiencing. What will be talked about next week? If it is the Saturday midnight story, teens won't want to be home by 11:30.

3. **Other People's Opinions:** Just as Other People's Opinions may block our growth from healthy risk-taking, they often encourage our willingness to take reckless risks.

4. **The Thrill:** Teens are natural thrill seekers. The energy thrill from reckless risks makes them feel alive.

5. **It's Fun:** Some of the things that are really in their Worst Interest are often seen as fun, enjoyable or pleasurable. The short term fun or pleasure, sooner or later, results in serious negative consequence.

6. **Bonding in Pain:** Teens crave meaningful social relationships. Unfortunately, many of these relationships are created through negative actions or reckless risks: "I'll do anything if it means I'm accepted into the group."

SELF-RESTRAINT AND SELF-DISCIPLINE

Top 20s have uncanny abilities to analyze a situation quickly and effectively make decisions based on their long-term Best Interest. Many times these decisions involve self-restraint and self-discipline.

Consider the examples of a healthy risk (trying out for the speech team) and unhealthy risk (driving a motorcycle without a license). Both may provide new experiences outside your Comfort Zone, but Top 20s ask three important questions before taking a risk.

1. Do I have to lie about what I'm doing?
2. What is the worst thing that could happen?
3. Can I live with that outcome?

How would you answer these questions regarding

- doing a class project with someone you don't know?
- experimenting with drugs?
- running for Student Council?

- shoplifting?
- asking someone to a dance?
- having sex?

LEARNING FROM OTHER'S MISTAKES

Top 20s are able to get more good out of life and avoid more of the pain because they learn from the mistakes of others. A Top 20 and a Bottom 80 both watch as a friend inserts a fork into an electrical outlet and gets a serious negative consequence. The difference? A Top 20 makes the observation that this is something he will not do. The Bottom 80 tries it himself, just to see if the results will be the same for him.

If you want to be a Top 20 in high school, look for the healthy risks and start taking them. As you take healthy risks it causes you to grow and develop Star Qualities to become a Top 20. Furthermore, learn from observing the reckless risks of Bottom 80s and be grateful for all the senseless pain you will avoid in your life.

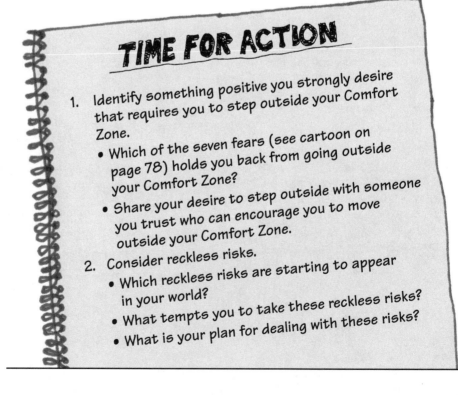

TIME FOR ACTION

1. Identify something positive you strongly desire that requires you to step outside your Comfort Zone.
   - Which of the seven fears (see cartoon on page 78) holds you back from going outside your Comfort Zone?
   - Share your desire to step outside with someone you trust who can encourage you to move outside your Comfort Zone.

2. Consider reckless risks.
   - Which reckless risks are starting to appear in your world?
   - What tempts you to take these reckless risks?
   - What is your plan for dealing with these risks?

LEARNING
"SCHOOL-SMART"

We believe school is really important in your life. A third of your life is currently spent having this experience. This includes what you're learning in your classes, your relationships with teachers and peers and your involvement in extracurricular activities. Using **"school-smarts"** will make this a wonderful experience for you.

Yet, we know that some of you are bored with school or not getting out of it what you would like. If that's the case for you, we believe it can improve. If school is already a positive experience for you, it can still get better. No matter what experience you've had until now, by applying what you learned in the Thinking section and what you will learn in this section, we believe there's a greater school experience in your immediate future.

"School-smart" is not a checklist of study skills tips. Rather, it's a way to look at learning as a life-long participation in relevant activities with more meaningful results.

Top 20s know there's more to school than grades, even though grades are the scale by which you are normally judged. As important as grades may be, the realizations and Star Qualities that are available during your school experience are also tremendously important. We don't want you to miss out on these even if you're already getting great grades. Like an iceberg there's much more below the surface that you are able to achieve regardless of your academic ability.

High school is an opportunity for you to practice all sorts of things to get better at being the person you are. We want you to take those healthy risks that will stretch you toward your best and truest self so you won't look back to your high school years, as many adults do, with feelings of regret for missed opportunities.

Seize the opportunities. Let school be your lab for experimenting and practicing what you're learning in this book as you embark on the wonderful adventure of becoming you.

GRADES

REALIZATIONS

STAR QUALITIES

What's in It for Me?

Have you ever thought or said any of the following statements?

"This is pointless."
"When am I ever going to use this?" ← *Math Class*
"This is irrelevant. It doesn't pertain to my life."

It is quite normal to have these thoughts during your school day.
But what effect do these thoughts have on your experience and, more
importantly, are they in your Best Interest? Do they ever block you from
having a positive experience and gaining something important?

HERE ARE TWO TRUTHS	
IT IS TRUE that if we spend our time talking about boring and pointless things we will unknowingly push ourselves deeper into the world of boredom.	**IT IS TRUE** that there is often relevancy in things we think are irrelevant. One of the biggest mistakes we make is that if we don't see the relevancy in something, we assume it's not there.

GETTING THE POINT OF POINTLESS

relevancy - the quality or state of being closely connected or appropriate.

Let's look for the truth about where relevancy can be found in those
classes that you think are irrelevant. When you wonder, "What is the
point of a class that I see as pointless?" ask yourself, "What's in it for me?"

The relevancy of a math class can be that it will help you with science in the future.

**The relevancy of an irrelevant class is not always to be found only in
the subject matter or the content.**

Christina says, "I'm not going to be a scientist. I don't see the value today
or in the future of understanding the elements in chemistry."

There is relevancy in understanding the concepts of science but those
who don't see that will think that science is totally irrelevant. Top 20s
have X-ray vision. They see something Bottom 80s don't see. Bottom 80s
look at the subject matter and say, "There's no point in this.

There's no value in this." Top 20s may not find relevancy in the content either but **they do find relevancy in the process of**

- **going** to chemistry every day.
- **learning** the elements.
- **doing** the reading at night.
- **raising** their hand in class.

"Sometimes in school it feels like grades are small rewards for performing tasks, just like throwing fish heads to a seal at the zoo. Now I know there's something bigger than grades. If I'm getting a D in math and really don't like the class but keep going and don't quit, I'm getting qualities out of the class that are much more important than the grade."
– E. J.

✳ Value is to be found not solely in the elements of chemistry but **by engaging** in chemistry class.

So you need to **look for the point or the value in the process**. You have got to have X-ray vision to see what's behind the process. What the process makes of you is the value. Top 20s know that in order for them to **evolve**, they must get **involved**.

[handwritten margin note: Summary — In order to find relevancy you must have "X-ray vision" and look beyond the process]

INTELLECTUAL MUSCLE

Christina knows darn well that she will not be a chemist but has decided to engage in the process of her chemistry class every day.

QUESTION: What does she have when the semester is over that she didn't have when it began?

ANSWER: Stronger Intellectual Muscle.

Even though you may not have liked chemistry, your active participation developed stronger Intellectual Muscle. Chemistry is the between-the-ears weightroom that provides you with the exercises that develops mental strength.

✳ Life is one big game of problem solving. Pick a job you think is cool-- astronaut, newscaster, fashion designer. All of these jobs require Intellectual Muscle to solve problems. Top 20s see the connection between developing this mental power and effective problem solving. For Bottom 80s that idea goes right over their head. Because they don't see the relevancy, they believe it doesn't exist.

[handwritten margin note: Ex: defining a problem and solving it using a plan]

"I once found science class incredibly irrelevant and boring. From TLC I now see that even though I may never use science when I'm older it's developing intellectual muscle in me now. Even though I don't feel like doing the work, I need to since it will help me develop discipline and perseverance."
– Phil

SUCCESS THAT FAILS...FAILURE THAT SUCCEEDS

In order to succeed, you need to have Star Qualities

The process known as school also offers you the Star Qualities that Top 20s are always seeking. When presented earlier (page 7) in the book, little mention was made about exactly how to acquire these characteristics. Wouldn't it be wonderful if you could get Star Qualities at the local fast food restaurant? You could just pull up at the drive-through and order what you'd like.

WELCOME TO STAR QUALITIES

SIDES:
COURAGE
TRYING AGAIN

SELF CONFIDENCE
SELF MOTIVATION
SELF DISCIPLINE
DECISION MAKING
...KING QUESTIONS
...KING CHARGE

Welcome to Star Qualities!

Hi, I'd like a double order of self-motivation, super-size my self-confidence and hold the boredom.

"I used to think that most of my classes were stupid and pointless. Now I see that Math teaches me to be persistent and make good use of my time. Biology makes me more organized, committed and focused."
– Tara

But not everything is as easy as ordering a burger and fries. Nonetheless, these extraordinary Star Qualities are available and attainable in daily life through your extra-curricular activities, family experiences, job and social life. Perhaps the best place to acquire these traits is at school.

Is it possible for a student to do well in a class, but not develop any Star Qualities? Yes.

Consider the examples of Miguel and Elena.

EXAMPLE

Miguel gets an A in science class but develops no Star Qualities. Why is this? Science is easy for Miguel. He doesn't have to put much effort into getting a good grade.

Elena gets a C- in science but develops three Star Qualities. The challenge of science requires her to become more organized, more persistent in asking for help, and more focused during class or study time. Why does this happen? Elena works harder.

When their science teacher writes letters of recommendation to colleges for these two students, the teacher will include several Star Qualities in Elena's letter but will struggle to find any for Miguel's.

Beyond her letter of recommendation, Elena's Star Qualities that are partially developed in science class are with her for life. As a mother, Elena will need to be **organized** in scheduling her children's activities, **persistent** in getting an electrician to come to her house when the furnace isn't working, and continually **focused** on her family's Best Interest. These qualities will also help her be successful in her work outside the home.

Star Qualities stay with you long after chemistry class is over. They hang out with you for the rest of your life and make a much larger difference in the quality of your life than just IQ. This doesn't mean that IQ isn't important. It does mean that EQ is more important in helping you create a good ride through school, relationships and life.

We discussed problem solving earlier, focusing on professional problem solving that would occur in all jobs. What about personal problem solving? What about decisions that need to be made regarding your family and friends, your future or your health? You need a variety of Star Qualities if you are going to succeed. Where do you get these? School is one place. It's an obstacle course you go through in order to pump up your muscles.

> "I didn't see the point of doing equations I would never use again in my lifetime. But after the TLC relevancy class I realize that the parabola I was doing may help me be a more patient person. Being a more patient person may help when I'm married and my husband shows up late for our Valentine's Day dinner."
>
> – Lindsey

IS IT JUST SCHOOL THAT'S POINTLESS?

Many students mistakenly believe that irrelevancy will disappear once they graduate. Unfortunately, it doesn't happen that way.

TRUE TALES

Some years ago Michael met Lee, a high school student who was totally disengaged in his classes. He believed that school was pointless. Michael asked him if he always thought school was pointless.

"No," Lee said, "school was OK until fourth grade."

"What happened in fourth grade?" asked Michael.

"I started feeling bad. And when I started feeling bad, I got scared. And when I got scared, I started feeling dumb. And then I realized that if I said school was pointless and I didn't care anymore, then I wouldn't feel dumb and no one would know I was scared."

What do you want to follow you after high school graduation? Do you want boredom and pointlessness to be part of your life? Lee had a job and a girlfriend after high school. He once shared with Michael that his job was pointless and his girlfriend was boring. Chances are you would prefer Star Qualities to follow you after high school. What a difference they would have made in Lee's life.

Star Qualities could make your life enjoyable.

The lesson that this young man's painful life teaches us is that we have to be careful about what we believe because what we believe can lock us in…permanently.

Summary
Staying engaged and having Star Qualities may teach you alot, but it doesn't end after school, they carry into your everyday life.

TIME FOR ACTION

1. Think of a class you currently see as pointless.
2. Consider the Star Qualities (see page 7) you want to develop.
3. How does engaging in the process of this class help you develop the Star Qualities you desire?

Roadblocks to Success

Consider the Star Qualities presented earlier in this book. We believe that you already have all of these qualities but something is in your way preventing their being expressed. Negative mental habits are blocking your Star Qualities. Some of these negative mental habits are listed below.

Pick three of these negative mental habits that are roadblocks for you.

- **Anger:** annoyed, mad
- **Judgmental:** critical of self or others
- **Grudges:** hanging on to ill will towards others
- **Sarcasm:** mean-spirited cutting remarks
- **Self-centered:** think only about self, inconsiderate of others
- **Jealousy:** envy, overly desiring another's traits or possessions
- **Apathy:** loss of will to care
- **Procrastination:** putting things off to the last minute
- **Pessimism:** anticipating negative results

- **Boredom:** having no interest
- **Worry:** anxious, troubled, uneasy, nervous
- **Self-doubt:** unsure of self, feeling inadequate
- **Mean:** bad tempered, malicious, unkind

LAW OF MENTAL HABITS

Think of these negative mental habits as heavy bags holding down your hot air balloon. As long as these bags are full of negative mental habits, your balloon cannot rise. If you apply the Law of Mental Habits, your Star Qualities balloon will soar.

LAW OF MENTAL HABITS
If you eliminate or reduce a negative mental habit,
positive mental habits will grow and flourish.

We're not saying it's easy to dump these bags. But how would it change your life if your negative mental habit bag weighs 20 pounds and you cut a hole in the bag to allow five pounds of negativity to drain out?

How can you do this in a practical and effective way?

"TLC made me recognize the inside flaws I have that I had chosen to hide. I am not done growing. I have a lot of things I want to change about myself yet. I now refuse to settle for anything less than what I deserve and what I think I can become."
– Kelly

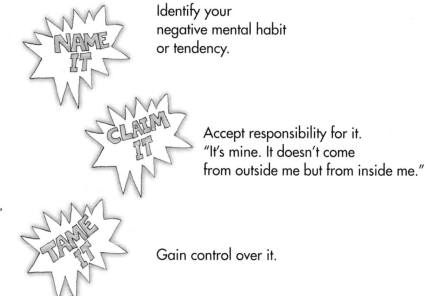

Identify your
negative mental habit
or tendency.

Accept responsibility for it.
"It's mine. It doesn't come
from outside me but from inside me."

Gain control over it.

Have you ever tried to get better at something only to have your bad habit come back? Why work on it if it's going to come back? If you are working on eliminating your anger, you might experience that it keeps coming back. But if you continue to be aware of it and work on it, when it returns it comes back with less intensity. It has a bit less control over you and you have a bit more control over it.

OUR BIGGEST OBSTACLES

Time after time our students rank two negative mental habits as their toughest personal obstacles or most harmful habits. If schools gave awards, many students would letter and even get All-State recognition for **boredom** and **procrastination**. Let's take a look at these common roadblocks to success.

"I'M BORED"

What do you find boring? Before you read any further take a moment to consider a situation in your life that you find boring.

Whether you're a Top 20 or a Bottom 80, you will experience boredom. Like most things in their lives, Top 20s deal with it differently than Bottom 80s. Top 20s apply the Inside/Outside Rule and take responsibility for their experience of boredom. Bottom 80s simply blame someone else or the situation and, therefore, stay stuck in boredom.

Remember the Inside/Outside Rule?

Most (90%) of your success or happiness is tied to your inside world—your thinking. Very little (10%) of your success or happiness is tied to your outside conditions.

The Inside/Outside Rule applies to boredom as well. Therefore, boredom (and the pain that comes with it) comes from your own head. Your boredom is determined by how you see something.

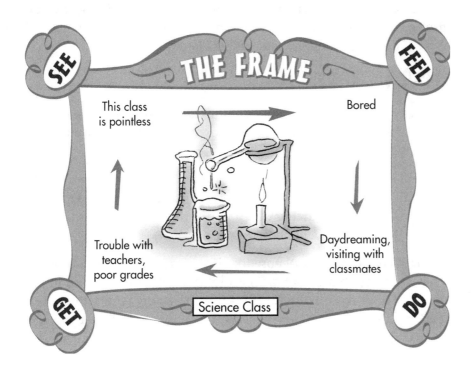

EXAMPLE

Duane is bored when he goes to church. Because his brothers and dad are bored after a particular church service, Duane is convinced that the source of his boredom is outside of himself—the church service.

If Duane is right, then there is nothing he can do about boredom short of changing the church service itself. But Duane is unaware that boredom is caused by a certain way of thinking. If he were aware of this, he could control his thinking and reduce boredom.

BOREDOM IS A BUSY MIND

Imagine your thinking being measured by the speedometer of a car. Sometimes your thinking can be going very fast—100 mph. Sometimes your thinking slows down—20 mph. **The faster your thinking is going, the more prone you are to be bored.**

This is different than what most people think. The common belief is that when you are bored your mind is going slower. But a very active mind is creating energy. Because you may be sitting in school you can't fully express that energy. **That's why common indicators of boredom are expressions of energy like doodling, finger drumming, pen tapping, knee bouncing, hair twirling, pen chewing, day dreaming and staring into space.** All of these are signs of an inability to sit still. They are little ways of burning off energy in a restless body.

REDUCING BOREDOM

Once you see that the cause of boredom is in your head, you can cure it. If you know how to control and improve your thinking, you can reduce your boredom.

You will experience boredom when you are thinking fast and you can't physically move to express your energy. Sitting still comes with the turf in most schools. By **slowing down your thinking** in these situations you will decrease your level of boredom.

"Before TLC I was frequently bored. Now when I get bored I tell myself, 'Not now. I need to pay attention,' and I tune back into the speaker."
– Stephanie

It is much easier to control boredom if you are aware of it when it begins. Once it gets full-blown out of control it is much more difficult to manage. You need to **be aware of your thinking and know when it begins to speed up.** As if you are driving a car, you have much better control of the car when you are going 30 mph than when you are going 90 mph.

Likewise, you will have a much better chance of controlling your thinking when it is going slower than when it is going faster.

This is like the beginning of a concert.

The first music you hear comes from the piccolo...

...this is followed by the flute section...

...and soon a hundred musicians have joined in and the music becomes powerful.

The time to stop this from reaching a crescendo is at the beginning when only the piccolo is playing.

> **Remember that the more you say you are bored, the more boredom you will feel. You can quickly create a boredom tornado by telling three friends how bored you are with your math class.**

One way to reduce boredom is to **practice the Ease Up technique.** If you think a class is extremely boring, Ease Up on the intensity of your feeling bored and think of it as a little less boring. Go from a nine to a six on the Conviction Scale. Say **"Maybe** it's boring" or "There **migh**t be something interesting here if I engage."

If you can Ease Up on how strongly you feel bored and slow down your mind, your boredom will be greatly reduced.

```
NOT BORED    CONVICTION SCALE    REALLY BORED
   1   2   3   4   5   6   7   8   9   10
```

BOREDOM CAN BECOME A LIFE-LONG MENTAL HABIT

Boredom is a mental habit. It is not caused by geography (where you are) or by the activity or lack of activity of people around you. As such, if you are bored in the here and now, you will probably take boredom into the next chapter of your life.

Michael was bored through most of high school. He believed that once he got out of school his boredom would disappear. Three years after high school Michael was still bored. He had been looking for situations to relieve his boredom, not knowing that the cause of his boredom was not in front of his eyes but behind his eyes. The source of his boredom was in his own mind.

When people take boredom into the next chapter of their lives, they sometimes seek unhealthy ways of dealing with this negative mental habit. The appeal of alcohol and drugs is that they provide temporary relief when people are bored. Gambling and over-spending are other symptoms of bored adults.

Students' habits (pen-clicking, doodling, daydreaming) in dealing with boredom are costly regarding grades and realizations in school. **The costs get even bigger** (serious credit card debt, alcohol and drug abuse, failed relationships) when they are carried into adult life.

Michael once worked with a man who owed $80,000 in credit card debt.

"Why do you have so much debt?" Michael asked.

"Well, I go shopping at the malls. I bought a big screen TV and I upgraded my computer."

"Why do you go there?"

"I go there because I'm bored," the man replied.

FAKE IT 'TIL YOU MAKE IT

If you are experiencing boredom in a particular class, try 'faking it". Faking it is doing the things students engaged in the class do even when they don't feel engaged.

- Sitting in the front of the class
- Keeping your eyes on the teacher and listening
- Asking a question 20 minutes into the class
- Doing homework for that class first each night

At the very least, commit to fully engaging for the first and last five minutes of each class. You may be surprised to find yourself engaged for the entire class period.

"One bored ninth grader of mine decided to use the first five minute technique and paid attention in a math class that he was failing. After one week he told me he was now connecting in class. He raised his grade from a low D to a B in just a few weeks."
– Pat (high school teacher)

If you don't know how to fake it in a particular situation or class, watch someone who is genuinely engaged in that situation.

Remember, **if you can't think your way into right acting, act your way into right thinking**. Act like you're not bored and it will reduce your boredom.

"My friend and I usually didn't participate in class so we decided to set up a point system to see what would happen. If you raised your hand and gave a relevant answer, you got one point. This got both of us to answer more in class."
– Dan

FAKE IT 'TIL YOU MAKE IT

TLC

PROCRASTINATION

Procrastination is putting off something that is unpleasant or burdensome. It could be unpleasant to apologize to your neighbors because your loud music has awakened their baby. It could be burdensome to dig out the car after a heavy snowfall. Other things you might procrastinate about are

- homework, especially long term projects.
- cleaning your room.
- mowing the lawn.
- calling people back if it's going to be unpleasant.

The benefit of procrastination is that it feels good. It feels good not to do that which is unpleasant or burdensome. However, the good feeling only lasts for a short time.

IUTGAWI

IIIUUTGAAAWIII!

"I Used To Get Away With It" is a major source of reinforcement for procrastination. Many times a sixth grade student puts off work until the last minute, then finds either

- a parent willing to cover for him

- a sympathetic teacher willing to extend the deadline or accept mediocre work.

High school and college are less conducive to "successful" procrastination. The real world is even less willing to comply with last minute efforts. The Internal Revenue Service and credit card companies penalize procrastinators with late fees. The airlines have an even more direct consequence: flights leave on time with or without procrastinators on board.

THE HIDDEN COST OF PROCRASTINATION

The down side of procrastination is that the unpleasant thing you put off still has to be done. Having put it off until the last minute means you now have to rush to get it done. Besides the last-minute work that comes with procrastination, a number of feelings of stress also tag along.

Check out the chart below to see how much work and stress it costs Thomas and Jackson to complete an assignment. Imagine that a social studies report is assigned that requires five hours of work. Thomas does no work on the first four days and five hours on the fifth day. Jackson does five hours of work on the first day and is done with the assignment.

Though both did five hours of work, their stress levels were different. Thomas doesn't have any stress on the first day. He hasn't thought about the project at all. On the second day his friends are talking about the project during lunch. Thomas is a bit embarrassed (one level of stress) because he hasn't gotten started yet. On the third day he feels some anxiety (two levels) because there are only two days left. Thomas feels a lot of frustration and stress (four levels) on the fourth day because, having a baseball game after school and other school assignments to do that night, he's unable to spend any time on social studies. On the fifth day he's feeling overwhelmed (six levels) for putting the project off but he finally completes it (five hours) well after midnight. The next day he's tired and crabby (eight levels) at work because he didn't get enough sleep. The cost of Thomas' procrastination is 26 units: 5 hours + 21 levels of stress.

Jackson, on the other hand, does the project (5 hours) on the first day. He has no stress, worry or anxiety for the rest of the week. His total cost is five units. Obviously, Jackson's experience was less costly.

"We had a four-day weekend and I had lots of homework. I didn't want to do what I always do and put it off until the last day, but on a Friday night I really didn't want to be doing all my homework. I decided to pace myself and do a little bit at a time. I would tackle one assignment every day so I wouldn't have to do it all at once late at night. It took a little self-discipline to pull out a book on a Saturday, but I just figured that I was going to do the same amount of work no matter when I did it. I'd rather do it when I wasn't all stressed out."
– Mary

COST OF PROCRASTINATION		DAY 1	DAY 2	DAY 3	DAY 4	DAY 5	DAY 6	TOTAL
Thomas	Hours of Work	0	0	0	0	5	0	5
	Stress Level	0	1	2	4	6	8	21
Jackson	Hours of Work	5	0	0	0	0	0	5
	Stress Level	0	0	0	0	0	0	0

DWANNAs AND DFLIs

If you are a procrastinator, you are distracted by everything. You are supposed to cut the lawn but you notice your third grade diary on the shelf in your room. So off you go into the diary and forget about the lawn. The same diary had been on the shelf the day before when your friend was over. Because you were enjoying having your friend over, you didn't even notice the diary.

Procrastination usually takes one of two forms: DFLIs or DWANNAs.

—"It's time to cut the grass...but I **D**on't **F**eel **L**ike **I**t."

—"Better get started on my homework project...but I **D**on't **Wanna.**"

If you procrastinate cutting the grass because you don't feel like it, then you are justifying not cutting the grass until you feel like it. So you wait and wait and wait until you feel like it. When will you feel like cutting the grass? You're never going to feel like it. It's like waiting at a bus stop until the bus comes by that is loaded with motivation for cutting grass. When that bus comes by, you'll get on. But have you ever seen that bus? No, of course not, because that bus is not on the route of life.

If your mother sat on this bench waiting to feel like changing your diaper when you were a baby, how long do you think you would have worn that diaper? Probably until you were old enough to take it off yourself.

Do Top 20s ever feel like not doing something? Sure. Do they wait for the bus that will change how they feel? Top 20s know there is no such bus. That's a big difference between Top 20s and Bottom 80s. Top 20s don't wait for something they know isn't going to happen.

Imagine Tiger Woods needing to practice his putting. After Tiger has breakfast, his caddy knocks on the door and says, "Tiger, let's go. Time to practice your putting."

Tiger responds with a DFLI, "Don't feel like it."

Do you think there's ever a day when Tiger doesn't feel like practicing. Absolutely. What does he do when he doesn't feel like it. He practices. Top 20s have DFLIs but they are not governed by DFLIs. The Bottom 80s are controlled by DFLIs.

Now you know one more reason why Top 20s develop Star Qualities and the Bottom 80s don't.

ACTION PRECEDES MOTIVATION

Let's say you have to do a big project on ants for your science class. Unless you really love ants, you are probably not going to feel like doing this project. If you start your assignment on ants by getting out the poster board, markers and pictures of ants, you will tap into your motivation to complete the project.

Top 20 Thinking

If I don't feel like it, I will do it anyway because doing it is in my Best Interest.

The solution to procrastination is jump in. Start. Often the little bit of energy it takes to get started is all that it takes to overcome procrastination. **Getting started generates motivation and provides you with the energy to complete the task.** Once you get the lawn mower out of the garage and start it you are very likely to finish cutting the grass.

Bottom 80 Thinking

If I don't feel like it, I won't do it.

The Coles often walk early in the morning but they never feel like getting out of bed at 5:00 a.m. If they waited until they felt like walking early in the morning, they would never walk. However, once they get outside and start moving it feels good to be walking. Now they are motivated to keep walking. Once you act, motivation will keep you acting. **Motivation comes in the doing.**

STAR QUALITIES vs. NEGATIVE MENTAL HABITS

Do you see how the two big negative mental habits of boredom and procrastination are related to Star Qualities? Remember the Law of Mental Habits at the beginning of this chapter:

If you eliminate or reduce negative mental habits, positive mental habits (Star Qualities) will grow and flourish.

All of the Star Qualities have an opposite negative mental habit. If the negative mental habit is reduced, the Star Quality is increased.

— If boredom goes down, focus goes up.
— If procrastination goes down, motivation goes up.

Top 20s know that they gain a double victory by defeating a negative mental habit. Not only do they eliminate a negative force in their life, but they also develop a Star Quality, a positive force in their life. You deserve the same. Go for it!

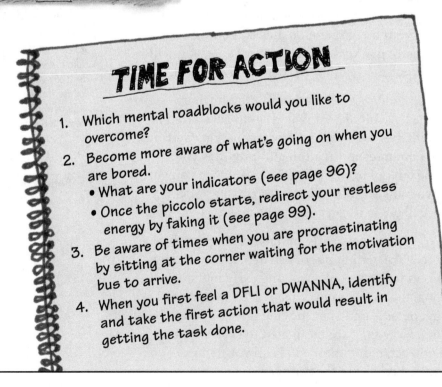

TIME FOR ACTION

1. Which mental roadblocks would you like to overcome?

2. Become more aware of what's going on when you are bored.
   • What are your indicators (see page 96)?
   • Once the piccolo starts, redirect your restless energy by faking it (see page 99).

3. Be aware of times when you are procrastinating by sitting at the corner waiting for the motivation bus to arrive.

4. When you first feel a DFLI or DWANNA, identify and take the first action that would result in getting the task done.

Levels of Listening

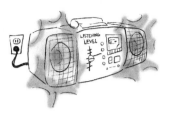

Have you ever sat through a one hour class but after the bell rang you were unable to recall any of the important ideas that were presented? Instead you were focused on

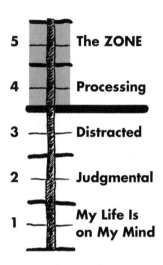

5 — The ZONE

4 — Processing

3 — Distracted

2 — Judgmental

1 — My Life Is on My Mind

- what you were going to do this weekend.
- how boring the teacher was.
- how hot the room was.

Top 20s know that **the secret to learning is effective listening.** Like most people, Bottom 80s believe they are good listeners. However, there's much more to listening than meets the ear.

First, not all listening is the same. We are going to identify five different levels of listening which indicate if a person is Above or Below The Line. Top 20s know when they are listening at the three levels Below The Line and how to change their listening to more effective Above The Line levels.

Using the three levels that are Below The Line will prevent effective listening. Using the two levels that are Above The Line will keep you focused, attentive and effective.

LEVEL 1: MY LIFE IS ON MY MIND

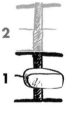

2

1

You're in the first level when you are focused on your own life and what you've got going on. You can be thinking of positive things like the fun you had at the lake last summer or the upcoming dance this weekend. You might be focused on a negative thought, like the argument you had with your mom this morning or the incomplete assignment that is due next hour in science class.

When you are listening with **My Life Is On My Mind** you are really listening only to yourself. This isn't a problem unless there is something else going on that requires your attention. This is the case with most of your school day. You're held accountable for the classroom material whether your life is on your mind or not.

Another part of My Life Is On My Mind is Fantasyland, that place you go when you're bored. Your Fantasyland might be attending a concert or replaying last night's soccer game or pretending that you're Superman. The result is not understanding the teacher's lecture and not enjoying the class experience. You get a bad grade and have a bad ride.

One way of dealing with the problem of My Life Is On My Mind and refocusing on the speaker is to temporarily put your thoughts in the **Parking Lot.** This means that you make a decision to put your thoughts aside until a later time. You want to consider these thoughts but **NOT NOW.**

The following illustration shows how a Top 20 student handles this during a science lecture.

Thinking about the phone call from Roy is more interesting to her but if she doesn't get what her teacher is saying she'll have more difficulty with her lab project. So she decides to put her thoughts about Roy in the **Parking Lot** until after school.

LEVEL 2: JUDGMENTAL

Not far from My Life Is On My Mind is a town called Judgmentville. This is a small-minded town with a huge population. Frank, a kid in the frog class, lives in Judgmentville. Let's see what's on his mind during his teacher's demonstration.

While Frank's judging his teacher, his classmates and himself, he's missing the teaching about the body parts of the frog. Are there going to be questions on the frog test about Frank's judgments of his teacher or classmates? That's the kind of question Frank's studying for when the real test question is going to ask him to label the body parts of the frog.

Being judgmental can include

- jumping to conclusions.
- over-reacting.
- interrupting or finishing other people's sentences.
- agreeing or disagreeing.
- evaluating self or others.

"In math class during homecoming week I didn't want any more homework than I already had. So I just concentrated as hard as I could. I didn't think judgmentally and suddenly didn't hear anything in my head. All I was thinking about was my worksheet in front of me and then, before I knew it, I was done and everyone else was still working."
– Sam

Unless you want to become a permanent resident in Judgmentville, you need to put these thoughts or reactions in the Parking Lot. Say, "Not now. I can always dislike this class or frogs later."

LEVEL 3: DISTRACTED

3

2

This level relates to those times when you are distracted by something in your environment. This could include a noise that you hear, observing what someone else is doing or a bee that just flew in the window. Sometimes what started out as an initial distraction can draw us into a Thought Circle or bring us to My Life Is On My Mind.

During the frog class Claire sees a fly that buzzes in the window and follows it to the other side of the room. It lands on Allison's back and begins to crawl across her shoulders. Again, the frog test will not include any questions about the use of flies in seeking revenge. Claire needs to park the fly thoughts and her feelings about Allison.

I wish that fly would crawl down her neck.

She deserves it what she said ab me when we wer the fifth grade

FROM TADPOLE TO FROG

Top 20s would also see the fly come in the window. Their response would be more like this: "Oh, a fly. NOT NOW." And back they would come to the frog class. Their distraction is brief and they get back on track much quicker.

The average person is distracted 22 minutes out of every 60 minutes. At least one-third of the time the average person is not focused on the task at hand. The classroom is full of tempting distractions: the clock, people walking by in the hall, the coughing kid, laughter from the classroom next door. If you are average you have lots of opportunities to practice "Not now."

Think of your learning success as being symbolized by a hot air balloon. Top 20s know that their learning balloon will not get off the ground when saddled with Below The Line listening habits.

JUDGMENTAL
DISTRACTED
LIFE ON MY MIND

LEVEL 4: PROCESSING

Processing is highly concentrated listening that is trying to analyze, memorize and synthesize all at the same time. Unlike the first three levels, this is more effective Above The Line listening. However, the problem with this level is that you are working so hard to be focused that you wear yourself out. Brain smoke will be coming from your ears. You will be exhausted by the end of class.

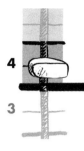

An example of process listening is a court recorder. This person writes down every word that is said during the trial. At the end of the trial the recorder would have no understanding of the proceedings but only an accurate written report. This same process occurs too often in the classroom.

Frogs are amphibians.

I know this stuff about the frog is going to be on the next test so I've got to listen carefully. Frogs are amphibians. Young frogs are tadpoles. Frogs are amphibians. Young frogs are tadpoles. Tadpoles. Amphibians.

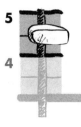

LEVEL 5: THE ZONE

It is only in **The Zone** that you get realizations about yourself, others and your class. Being in The Zone occurs when your mind is quiet and calm. In a sense, nothing is on your mind. You are totally present to the moment, living in the NOW. It's as if your mind is a dry sponge that is able to take in whatever the moment presents. When you are living in the other levels, you are living more in the past or the future. Your mind is like a soaked sponge. Anything in the present is just like adding more water to an already soaked sponge. Nothing is absorbed.

This presents a challenge. How can you keep your mind quiet when there is so much noise coming from the outside (**Distractions**) or the inside (**Judgmental** or **My Life Is On My Mind**)? How can you stay in the present when you find the past or the future so much more interesting?

By not listening in the first four levels your mind will revert to its most natural state, The Zone. Reminding yourself "Not now" and putting things in the Parking Lot will develop in you the mental habits to enter The Zone.

A young frog is called a tadpole.

WERE YOU LISTENING?

By simply cutting these "weights" from your basket, your balloon is going to rise dramatically. You will automatically move in the direction of the most effective level which you are naturally wired to do.

Now you know what Top 20s know:
the secret to better learning is better listening.

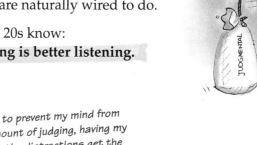

"The listening levels taught me to prevent my mind from wandering. Cutting down the amount of judging, having my life on my mind, and not letting the distractions get the best of me really helped to improve my grades and to be more aware of what is going on in class."
— Theresa

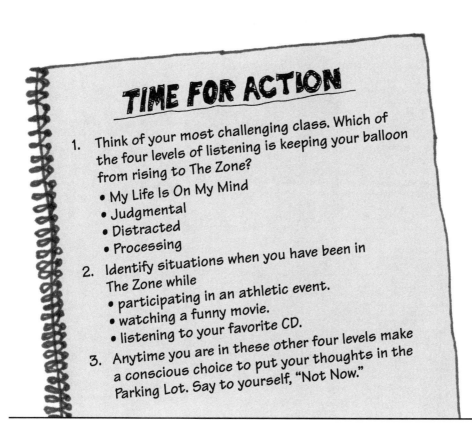

TIME FOR ACTION

1. Think of your most challenging class. Which of the four levels of listening is keeping your balloon from rising to The Zone?
   - My Life Is On My Mind
   - Judgmental
   - Distracted
   - Processing

2. Identify situations when you have been in The Zone while
   - participating in an athletic event.
   - watching a funny movie.
   - listening to your favorite CD.

3. Anytime you are in these other four levels make a conscious choice to put your thoughts in the Parking Lot. Say to yourself, "Not Now."

Realizations:
In The Moment & After The Fact

The ultimate goal of learning is achieving realizations, which occur when the light bulb goes on in your head and you exclaim, "Aha!" Realizations involve

- understanding principles.
- knowing the facts and underlying meaning of an event.
- knowing how to apply learning to real life situations.

Memorization is "Small Learning". Realizations are the "Big Learning" that renders memorizing unnecessary.

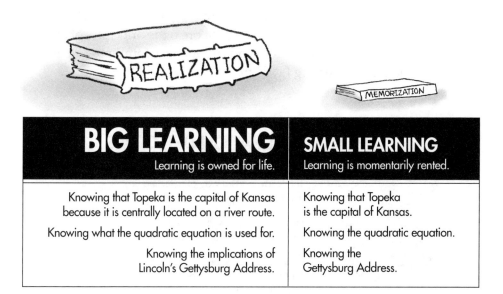

BIG LEARNING Learning is owned for life.	SMALL LEARNING Learning is momentarily rented.
Knowing that Topeka is the capital of Kansas because it is centrally located on a river route.	Knowing that Topeka is the capital of Kansas.
Knowing what the quadratic equation is used for.	Knowing the quadratic equation.
Knowing the implications of Lincoln's Gettysburg Address.	Knowing the Gettysburg Address.

Realizations are not usually graded in high school. A vast majority of classes in high school focus on Memory Learning or Small Learning. Life, however, especially the quality of life, is much more determined by realizations. Knowing the alphabet is of little value in life unless it can lead to reading and writing. This does not negate the importance of Memory Learning. Rather, we are urging you not to stop there.

"I got A's because I understood it, not because I memorized it."
– Jessi

Top 20s always go for realizations and Big Learning. They know that behind every subject in school is a principle, system or pattern to realize.

When Michael was a young boy his father was a taskmaster. He gave Michael multiplication flash cards and told him that every Friday night he would be tested on the table of the week. If Michael passed he would be allowed to go out and play on Saturday. The way he learned the weekly table was to say it out loud and memorize it: "3 x 4 is 12. 3 x 4 is 12. 3 x 4 is 12." All he wanted to be able to do was hold it in his head until Friday.

One day his father asked him if he understood how multiplying 3 x 4 can equal 12.

"No," Michael said.

"Then why are you doing this?"

"Because I want to play on Saturday. I want to pass the test."

What Michael was getting was only Small Learning. Through his memorizing he eventually had the realization of how multiplication worked. Suddenly he understood the principle of multiplication: $3 \times 4 = 3 + 3 + 3 + 3$. From that moment on he never had to memorize the remaining multiplication tables.

Unfortunately, Michael applied Small Learning in high school when he tried to memorize algebra. He never caught on to the principles of algebra. It wasn't until he was a 45-year old and sitting in on Tom's pre-calculus class that he experienced Big Learning.

REALIZATION DETECTORS

The following is a way of detecting if your learning is Big or Small.

Imagine that you will be tested on certain material that you are learning.

If you can devise memory techniques for the test, then what you are learning is Small Learning.

Realizations or Big Learning don't lend themselves to memory techniques.

FRONT PAGE NEWS

Extra, extra, read all about it!

Experts Discover Realizations Occur Two Different Ways...

IN THE MOMENT:
An understanding of the material as it is being presented.

AFTER THE FACT:
An understanding of the material that comes after the material has been presented.

In grade school, most realizations occur In The Moment (ITM). Almost everything in grade school is ITM. Teachers won't allow the class to go out for recess until everyone knows that the Statue of Liberty is located in New York. You'd be less likely to be sent home to discover that After The Fact (ATF).

ATF learning occurs frequently in college. Sometimes realizations don't come on the spot in the classroom or lab. A geology professor's lecture might be about a rock climbing expedition but what you are to learn on caves is assigned on pages 48-96 in the textbook. You will need to dig up the learning yourself. As we progress in school, a greater percentage of learning is expected to occur ATF.

The big news is that high school is the transition between grade school and college when it is expected that you take on greater responsibility for your learning. In high school, a growing amount of realizations will come during homework and study sessions. And if you haven't gotten a particular learning ITM, then you are responsible for getting it ATF.

This provides hope for lots of our students. They're not dumb just because the bell rang and they didn't understand all that the teacher presented. It doesn't mean they can't learn the material. They don't have to get trapped in a negative Thought Circle and think they're the only ones not getting it. **They just haven't gotten it Yet.**

ITM LEARNING	ATF LEARNING
GRADE SCHOOL	GRADE SCHOOL
75%	25%
HIGH SCHOOL	HIGH SCHOOL
50%	50%
COLLEGE	COLLEGE
25%	75%

"I think I now know why I did so poorly in grade school. I'm more of an ATF kind of person. I think I must be the worst person at memorizing. But now I'm getting better grades because there's more ATF learning in high school."
– Catherine

AN ATF MOTIVATOR

At the end of a class, you might say, "I didn't get it." In your mind that thought might discourage you from ever getting it. You've just told your brain to take the day off.

If you think this way, you need an ATF Motivator. Allow us to introduce you to **Yet** whose job it is to keep your brain thinking that learning is possible and probable. **Yet** will encourage you to find ATFs. When you become aware that you didn't learn something ITM, say, "I don't understand this, **Yet**."

There are some languages YET doesn't understand.
YET doesn't understand the language of Never and Can't.

I didn't get it and I'll never get it.

I don't get it **Yet**... but I'm not giving up 'til I get it.

It's too hard. I can't get this.

TRUE TALES

Paul's daughter Katie was a gymnast in grade school. At practice one night her coach asked, "Katie, can you do an aerial?" (An aerial is a cartwheel without putting your hands on the floor.)

"I haven't done one, **Yet**," Katie responded.

YET kept Katie believing in her potential to do an aerial. Sure enough, a few weeks later her body was performing what "Never" and "Can't" would not have allowed her to do.

ATF BUS STOPS

If you don't have an ITM, you need to immediately head
for one of the ATF bus stops. This bus doesn't stop for you when
you're sleeping, shopping at the mall, or watching TV.
It also doesn't stop when you believe

- "I'm really dumb."
- "She's smarter than I am."
- "My teacher is awful."

The ATF bus stops

- when you raise your hand
  and ask a question.

- at a study group of friends
  seeking Big Learning.

- when reviewing class notes
  and reading your textbook.

- while doing your
  homework in a focused
  and deliberate manner.

The point is if you didn't catch the
learning on the ITM bus, you're
responsible for catching the learning
on the ATF bus.

In college, Paul's roommate Tim could read a book in two hours that would take Paul eight or
more. Tim got some things quicker. Good for Tim. But it didn't matter that Paul didn't have the
book done in two hours. It simply meant he needed to take the ATF bus to the library for several
hours each night.

What will Top 20s do when they don't get it? We've already mentioned a
few things. They will catch an ATF bus and call upon Yet. But what if Big
Learning still isn't happening? Then they follow this rule:

> **Memorization (Small Learning)
> is often the pathway to Realization (Big Learning).**

Let's say that you don't have a deep understanding of parabolas and your teacher has written seven points about them on the board. You should write the seven points down in your notebook and memorize them at home.

Top 20s know that confusion precedes realizations. If you think that confusion means it's over and it's hopeless, then you will never get a realization. So allow yourself to keep going and you will eventually see the light.

Don't be confused by confusion.

Stay in the process.

Have faith.

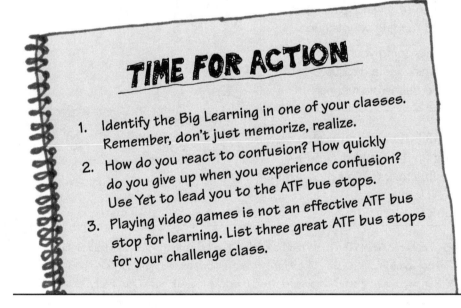

TIME FOR ACTION

1. Identify the Big Learning in one of your classes. Remember, don't just memorize, realize.

2. How do you react to confusion? How quickly do you give up when you experience confusion? Use Yet to lead you to the ATF bus stops.

3. Playing video games is not an effective ATF bus stop for learning. List three great ATF bus stops for your challenge class.

Organization For Success

Organization is a Star Quality. This is obvious when you become aware of the problems you experience in your life because of disorganization.

Have you ever been the victim of someone else's disorganization?

- Have you ever been left behind?
- Have you ever not had a phone call returned?
- Have you ever done a project with someone who didn't do her half of the workload?
- Did your Little League coach ever fail to turn in the roster for a tournament so your team was unable to participate?

"I was very unorganized all through grade school. When we started to learn about organizational skills in TLC class, I realized there is hope for unorganized people and have become more organized with my school stuff."
– Joe

Have you ever been the victim of your own disorganization?

- Have you ever misplaced an important phone number?
- Have you ever lost points on a long term assignment because you didn't turn it in on time?
- Have you ever wasted time looking for something because you didn't put it where it should be?
- Did you ever have to pay a late fee for a rented video?

The first thing you need to do to become better organized is to see organization as one of the big values. Remember **The Frame**. Only if you **see** that organization is valuable will you **feel** the desire to **do** those things that make you more organized so that you can **get** the results effective organization causes.

This chapter offers you some things to consider and some actions to take in order to enjoy the benefits of better organization.

KEEPING

Are you a keeper? Are you the kind of person that keeps movie stubs, a fourth grade Spanish quiz, pictures from summer camp, a letter from a friend and special quotes? Keeping is not the same as accessing. Can you access those things that you want or need when you want or need them? Can you access all your labs for the science class you're currently taking? Can you access all the social studies tests you've had this semester? Where do you keep your stuff? Can you get to it when you need it?

THE PLYWOOD RULE

Folks in South Carolina have three opportunities to put plywood over their windows during hurricane season: before, during, or after the hurricane. When would the most organized people put plywood on their windows? They would do it before the storm comes. If we relate this rule to school, it would apply to those students who study before the test.

But some people try to put plywood on the windows during the storm. They're usually being blown all over the place but they continue their struggle to get the plywood up. These would be students who study on their way into the room, or open their book or notes for two minutes before the bell rings.

The third group puts the plywood up after the storm when all the windows have been blown out. These would be students who fail the test and try to learn the material afterwards.

ORGANIZATIONAL DO'S

1. **Plan the fun stuff first.**
   Obviously this has to be balanced with other responsibilities but identify what you would enjoy during the next week and schedule that first. Make sure to include rest as part of your plan.

2. **Get in the habit of writing things down.**
   Don't just smile and nod when someone is giving you a list of things to learn or do. It doesn't matter if your system includes a planner, a date book, or notes on the refrigerator, as long as it works for you.

3. **Take a minute to organize your work load.**
   Do your least favorite homework first. Save your favorite subject for last and do the **worst first**. Schedule your most important work when you have the most energy to focus.

4. **Plan ahead**.
   Put the things you will need the next day out the night before so you don't have to be hunting for them in the morning when you're running late. These include clothes and school stuff (back pack, homework or permission slips).

5. **Have one centrally-located spot**.
   Keep little things that matter, like keys, wallet, watch and jewelry, in one spot.

   "I always forgot when things were due or when hockey practice was. Since I've been in TLC, I've bought a planner and now I know when hockey is."
   – Maddie

6. **Use a large calendar**.
   Record all the activities or events you or your family need to remember. Sometimes merely looking ahead will limit conflicts or problems.

Tom is one of those people who is on the extreme end of the organizational continuum. He religiously keeps a calendar date book to organize his life. He color-codes his "to-do" lists each day (yellow = school, blue = family; green = social; orange = financial). He uses a "circle" check list that he fills in after each task is completed.

The Cody shopping list is yet another extreme example. The menu for the next week is planned first. Then the necessary food items are written on the grocery list. Tom has organized this shopping list by the aisles at his local store to save time when searching for something.

21-DAY RULE

Studies show that it takes 21 days of practicing a new behavior for it to become a habit. What could you commit to doing for three weeks that would help you develop an organizational habit?

- Keep room clean
- Hang clothes up
- Be ready for school the night before
- Keep folders organized
- Throw away the stuff that you don't need
- Do homework right after school

One problem with the 21-Day Rule is the tendency to **fade**, which occurs when well-intentioned goals are replaced by former bad habits. You may set a goal of doing homework right after school but after doing this for a few days you resume your old habit of waiting until late at night.

Obstacles are sure to show up whenever we set a goal. Bottom 80s are often defeated by the first obstacle and quit. They fade to the old ways.

"What's the use? It doesn't work. I'll never get over this hurdle"

Top 20s get mentally tough when confronting the first obstacles. Their determination gets them over the early hurdles and gives them the confidence for more challenging obstacles. They're developing Star Qualities for the future.

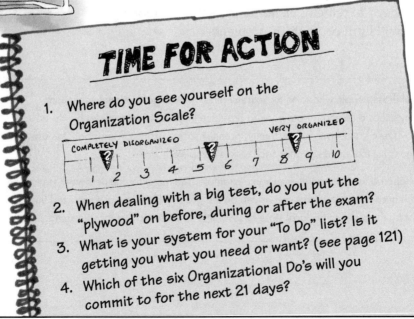

TIME FOR ACTION

1. Where do you see yourself on the Organization Scale?

   COMPLETELY DISORGANIZED | VERY ORGANIZED
   1 2 3 4 5 6 7 8 9 10

2. When dealing with a big test, do you put the "plywood" on before, during or after the exam?

3. What is your system for your "To Do" list? Is it getting you what you need or want? (see page 121)

4. Which of the six Organizational Do's will you commit to for the next 21 days?

Missing the Boat

Have you ever missed out on something that was important to you? Did your team win a big game when you were injured? Did your family have an enjoyable vacation when you didn't go? Did your friends have fun at a party when you stayed home? Did you fall behind in school because you were sick?

Missing the Boat means you are missing out on something you would benefit from if you were present. This could include missing an activity, being absent from class or a practice or not showing up for work.

Being absent from science class is equivalent to having the Science Ship leave with you left on the dock. You have missed the boat and it will never come back to pick you up. If you ever miss the boat, dive in quickly while you are just a little bit lost. Some students tend to wait and wait until they are hopelessly lost.

"High school is completely different than grade school. Missing one day in high school is like missing an entire week in grade school. There is so much you need to catch up on, not just the homework you were assigned the day you missed but how to do the homework."

– Lindsey

IN GRADE SCHOOL THE BOAT COMES BACK

If you missed a day of school in fifth grade because you were sick or deer hunting with your father, you have many repetitive things that you can do at home to catch up. You can go home on Tuesday with the things you missed in school on Monday and accomplish what the teachers want you to do to get caught up. You can usually make up your missed day easily because

- parents and teachers take an active role in getting your assignments to you.

- you usually possess the skill level to complete the task.

In high school you won't always have the skills, knowledge or content, nor can you draw easily from the text to accomplish the catching up. There's a bigger gap between you and the boat when you miss a class in high school. In grade school the boat pretty much comes back to the dock every day. It's as if there is a built-in system for picking up stragglers—like staying in for recess or lunch—but there's no such thing in high school.

In high school assume the boat is not coming back.

NOT ALL CLASSES ARE THE SAME

All is not lost. We do have some suggestions for you when you Miss the Boat. But first, let's clarify some points.

Missing the Boat is a BIG deal in almost all high school classes but it is bigger in some than in others. Some classes are extremely **sequential**. That means that you need to understand today's material before you're able to understand tomorrow's material.

— Monday's math class on linear equations is needed in order to understand quadratic equations on Tuesday and graphing on Wednesday.

— If you don't get "**-er**" **verbs** conjugation in Spanish, the next lesson on "**-ir**" **verbs** will be extremely difficult.

Some classes are more **nonsequential**. That means that each day stands alone or is less directly connected to the previous day's class.

— Participating in three days of volleyball in physical education class isn't likely to impact your performance in softball the next three days.

— Mastering a geography lesson on Chile will not have a great impact on the next day's lesson on Brazil.

THE ABSENT SHIELD

You may have picked up a great trick to protect yourself as a younger student—using the Absent Shield. Is this one of those old habits you used in grade school?

This shield develops whenever you get by without having work done because you were absent. In high school, use of this shield will protect you from learning. Your teachers know this trick and it angers them. **Using this shield in high school is not in your Best Interest.**

> I'm safe. My teacher can't expect me to be done with my assignment because I was absent yesterday.

TWO CYCLES

Attendance is directly connected to the quality of experience you will have in high school. The results (grades) and the ride will be significantly better if you attend school regularly.

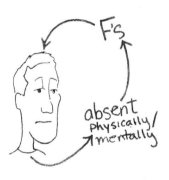

If you are absent from school, you tend to have poorer grades. Lower grades may tend to turn you off even more to school. You are now more likely to disengage mentally even if you are physically present. **Your body is in the desk but your mind is absent**. Now you're caught up in a cycle that leads to even worse grades.

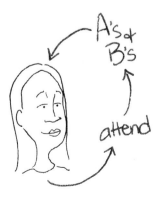

Top 20s create a different cycle. Because they are physically and mentally present, they get better grades. Because they are learning, they become more engaged in the class. This results in additional learning or even better grades.

> *"I sometimes missed 12 days in a trimester. I got to the big ugly cycle of missing school, failing and not coming to school because I was failing. I didn't want to go to school because of bad grades. I was deep in the cycle."*
> — Nancy

"I went on vacation with my family in the spring. I had been assigned to read 100 pages out of our literature book for class. I said I would read it and fill out the worksheets. I ended up reading about two pages."
— Dave

AVOID MISSING THE BOAT

Missing the Boat is an issue for everybody. Top 20 students have developed effective strategies to avoid Missing the Boat.

1. **Weigh the positives and negatives before making a decision to miss class**: Going on a family vacation in the winter to a warm climate means fun and sun. That's hard to pass up when staying home means a week of cold weather and school. The price for your short-term pleasure will be paid with long hours of work when you return. Use the same discretion when making doctor or dentist appointments.

2. **Half sick, half day rule**: Attend school for half a day if you're not contagious or so sick that you need to stay in bed. Consider attending those classes that are most critical for you.

3. **Make a schedule change of your own:** High school teachers usually teach the same class two or three times each day. If the class you are missing is taught at another time, consider getting permission to switch class periods that day.

STAYING AFLOAT WHEN MISSING THE BOAT

Sometimes missing school is unavoidable. If your older brother is getting married in another state, if you are attending a relative's funeral, or if you are just too darn sick, missing school can be the right thing to do. Top 20 students use **four** strategies for staying afloat when they have to Miss the Boat.

1. **Own the problem**: Take full responsibility for the absence and for making up the work. Never wield the Absent Shield.

2. **Be proactive**: If you know in advance that you are going to miss class, make arrangements with your teacher. Politely ask your teacher for options: assignment sheets, reading ahead, a copy of class notes, attending a class taught at a different time, meeting before or after school.

"I missed some classes due to family business . Thanks to TLC tips, I'm not scared to approach my teachers to see what I missed. In grade school I'd just say, 'I wasn't here' and I'd never even think of making up the work."
– Colin

Remember, it's not a teacher's responsibility to bring the boat back if you are standing on the dock. It's your job to figure out how to catch up to the boat.

The way you approach teachers will make a difference.

A Bottom 80's Approach

Hey! Miss Sweeney, are you gonna be doin' anything in history class next week? I'm going to the Bahamas. You gotta show me what I'm gonna miss.

A Top 20's Approach

Excuse me, Miss Sweeney. I'm going out of town with my family next week. I know it's up to me to handle what I miss. Is there anything I can do before I leave? What do I need to take care of when I get back?

3. **Connect with a reliable study buddy:** Find someone who can get you notes and other pertinent information (like when a test may be scheduled) from the class you will miss. Call your study buddy as soon as possible so you will know what you need to do.

4. **Attend support sessions:** Does your school or teacher hold after-school study sessions? Can you get help before school, during lunch or during a teacher's prep time? These are things you should know in advance of making a decision to Miss the Boat. If all else fails, get a private tutor if you miss several classes.

By following through in these ways you are not only working on learning the material but also developing the Star Quality of responsibility. Be assured that your teachers and parents will notice.

SCHOOL IS IMPORTANT

What we want you to learn from this chapter is that attending classes in high school is very important. If you must miss a class (like visiting the orthodontist), take Missing the Boat into account. Furthermore, minimize the damage of absences by taking responsibility for the material you will miss.

> Top 20s know how to be proactive and accountable.

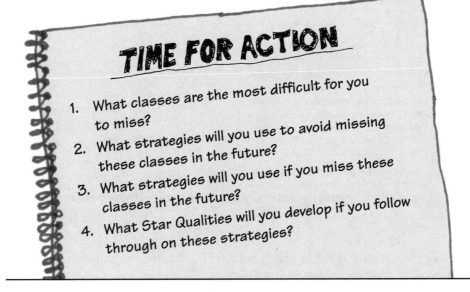

TIME FOR ACTION

1. What classes are the most difficult for you to miss?
2. What strategies will you use to avoid missing these classes in the future?
3. What strategies will you use if you miss these classes in the future?
4. What Star Qualities will you develop if you follow through on these strategies?

Goals:
Bettering Your Best

Top 20s have many secrets. One of them is knowing that tucked inside themselves is the potential to become better in some areas of their lives. Since their mission is to become the best they can be, the possibility of becoming better excites and motivates them. They also know that one of the best ways of unlocking that potential is to establish and work towards goals.

What are goals? **Goals are a powerful thinking and learning strategy for bettering your best.**

The number one reason why Olympic athletes reach such high levels of performance is because they have for a lifetime believed in the concept of "kaizen." This Japanese word means continual improvement—reaching your personal best and then trying to better it.

We are not stressing the importance of goals so you can become the best but so you can **better your best**. We're not stressing perfection but improvement. We're asking you to reach for your **All Time High**. We're asking you not to settle for "I'm OK," but to stretch for your great performance. Top 20s know there's one thing more important than being good and that's getting better.

When you stop getting better, you eventually stop being good.

SHOOT HIGHER, LAND HIGHER

For Top 20s to aim high and fail is better than to aim low and hit the mark. They know that the higher they shoot, the higher they land.

Example: Terry's goal is to read six books during the summer. If he only reads four, he's better off than having a goal of three books and attaining it.

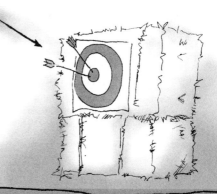

SETTING SMART GOALS

You need to be SMART in order to write effective goals because not all goals are helpful. In fact, some goals can keep you spinning your wheels and not getting anywhere. In order to be effective, your goals need to include five important characteristics:

Each of these characteristics will help you set achievable goals.
Let's take a look at each one.

SPECIFIC

The problem with some goals is that they are too vague. Wanting to be a better student or a better basketball player may be the outcome of goals but they are not goals in themselves. To be most effective, goals need to be specific.

Having a specific goal keeps your attention and energy very focused. If your goal is too vague, you will not know exactly where to direct your efforts.

VAGUE GOAL	SPECIFIC GOAL
To be a better math student.	To turn in all math homework.
To be a better basketball player.	To make layups with both my left and right hand.

MEASURABLE

By making your goal measurable, you are able to keep score and judge how you are doing. Measurable goals provide you with a way of getting feedback so you will know if you are progressing towards your goal.

"To turn in all math homework" is a very measurable goal. If you turn in your homework, you know you have achieved your goal; if you don't turn in an assignment, you know you haven't reached your goal.

Although shooting layups with both your left and right hand is measurable, it could be a more measurable goal by adding a percentage to it: to make <u>at least 80%</u> of my left-handed and right-handed layups.

As you practice layups you can keep track of the percentage you make and know if you are getting better.

Top 20s know the importance of keeping score; they are constantly measuring and evaluating in order to improve. If their goal is to meet three new people by Friday, they keep score. On Tuesday they met one new person. On Thursday they met a second new person. **Top 20s always know where they are in their effort to achieve their goal.**

Bottom 80s don't keep score. Why not? If you don't keep score, you can't fail. Bottom 80s fear failure so they don't keep score. Top 20s measure their progress because they don't fear failure. If they fail, they learn from that experience and do it better the next time. Failure is one form of feedback for Top 20s.

ACTION ORIENTED

A SMART goal also focuses on the action needed in order to achieve the desired results. Action oriented goals focus your attention and energy.

NON-ACTION ORIENTED	ACTION ORIENTED
To be a better math student.	To eliminate distractions and sit at my desk in order to complete all my math homework.
To be a better basketball player.	To work on left and right hand lay-ups for 15 minutes after practice.

REALISTIC

Because you are trying to improve, your goals are intended to stretch you, yet be within your reach. While unattainable goals will frustrate you, realistic goals will challenge and motivate you. It would be wonderful if you got a perfect score on all your math assignments or never missed a layup, but those goals are not realistic. Turning in all your assignments and making 80% of your layups are more realistic. It is not realistic for Tom Cody at age 50 to set a goal of joining a professional ballet troupe.

You also need to be realistic about the time it takes to reach a goal. It's unrealistic to set a goal of raising your grade in science from a C to an A if there's only one week left in the semester. It's more realistic to set that goal for the next semester.

TIME LIMITED

Setting a deadline for achieving your goals may help to avoid procrastination and motivate you toward your goals.

NOT TIME LIMITED	TIME LIMITED
To turn in all my math homework on time.	To turn in all of my math homework on time for the next three chapters.

Shoua and Matthew have identified something outside their Comfort Zone that they wish they could do. If they merely wish for these things to happen, they never will. So they have set SMART goals to achieve what they want.

Shoua would like to meet more people at school.
Shoua's SMART Goal: To introduce herself to three new classmates before lunch on Friday.

Matthew would like to be on the chess team.
Matthew's SMART Goal: To attend the informational meeting for the chess team on Monday after school.

Shoua and Matthew's goals are good examples of the SMART formula:

Specific + Measurable + Action oriented + Realistic + Time limited = Goal

WATCH OUT FOR THE THREE BEARS

What keeps Bottom 80s from setting and achieving SMART goals? The Three Bears.

Have you seen them yet? Have you noticed them lurking around whenever you consider setting a goal? They're the mental barriers that get in the way of your goals. They're known as Rationalizing Bear, Justifying Bear and Procrastinating Bear. Instead of eating honey, these bears devour goals. They want to eat up your dreams of bettering your best.

RATIONALIZING BEAR convinces you that something isn't very important. This can occur before setting a goal or after failing to achieve one. Sometimes Rationalizing Bear convinces you to not even set a goal.

Example 1: "Math is dumb anyway. My dad got C's. So what if I didn't do my homework? What's the big deal?"

Example 2: Miranda tries out for the play but doesn't make it. She rationalizes by saying: "What a stupid play. I'm glad I didn't make it. Look at the geeks who made it. I certainly don't want to hang out with them for three months."

JUSTIFYING BEAR is the excuse bear. Wally wants to go out for the debate team but finds an excuse not to.

Example: "I wanted to join the debate team but they sometimes practice on Saturday mornings and my sister's wedding is on a Saturday."

Although a debate coach would understand the importance of Wally attending his sister's wedding and excuse him from attending a practice, Wally has allowed Justifying Bear to get him off the hook. Who loses? Wally.

PROCRASTINATING BEAR takes your goals into hibernation. Along the road to success, Procrastinating Bear finds you a parking space where you put off acting in your Best Interest.

Example: Mia knows she needs to see her English teacher before turning in her long term project on Friday. After school on Tuesday she hangs out with her friends and never gets to her teacher. On Wednesday she hurries home after school to watch Oprah. When school's over on Thursday, Mia heads to the mall to do some shopping. As she turns in her project on Friday, she knows she hasn't completed all the requirements of the assignment.

Who loses? Mia, who parks along the road to success.

These three cute little bears encourage you to stay in your Comfort Zone. Although appearing to be your pals, they're certainly no friends of yours. They're simply holding you back from bettering your best.

FEAR NOT!

Fear is another great block to achieving our goals. Our fears disempower us from moving forward and strip us of our potential to better our best. Like the three cuddly bears, they're not sweet, innocent creatures; they're monsters.

Here are some of the big fears that can hold you up.

- Fear of failure or rejection
- Fear of humiliation or embarrassment
- Fear of Other People's Opinions
- Fear of success
- Fear of discomfort or change

"I made a goal of meeting three n. friends the first semester. I was having trouble because I was afraid rejection. I learned about OPOs ar changed my thinking. Once I got pa others' opinions, I made friends quic
– Armin

Remember, Top 20s know that **failure is an event, not a person**. They see failure as a temporary setback from which they can learn something that helps them discover the way to an ultimate success. Failure's not a parking place on the road to success but a road sign guiding you to finding the right route.

"If you want to be successful, double your failure rate."
—Tom Watson, president, IBM

Top 20s also know that Other Peoples' Opinions of them are none of their business. When Alphonso wants to try out for the chess team and a friend says, "That's dumb. Only weirdos are on the chess team," Alphonso responds, "OK, thanks for your opinion but I'm going to do it anyway." Alphonso is not going to be denied his goal by OPOs.

LEVELS OF COMMITMENT

Every goal that is worth striving for has some degree of struggle or adversity attached to it. Your ability to achieve a goal has a lot to do with your commitment. No goal will ever get accomplished without commitment.

These levels of commitment can be compared to climbing a mountain.

CLIMBER
High commitment:
"I'm in no matter what."

CAMPER
Some commitment:
"I'm in as long as it's easy."

QUITTER
No commitment:
"I'm out."

A Quitter looks at a challenge and says, "No way. I can't do that. It's too hard." A Camper looks at a challenge and says, "I want to do that and I'll stay with it as long as it's easy." A Climber looks at a challenge and says, "That's for me. I know I'll have to deal with some tough situations. I'm not sure what or how but I believe I can do it."

PERSISTENCE

Persistence, the ability to stick with it, is a Star Quality necessary for becoming a Top 20. On the road to success, it's vital to stay on that path. Top 20s use the WISE method to assure that they achieve their goals:

Will-power: Not succumbing to temptations; having self-discipline.

Initiative: Self-starting, using the power that comes from within you.

Stamina: The strength to continue when you're tired or don't feel like it.

Enthusiasm: Having the passion to achieve the goal; finding pleasure and enjoyment in the process.

GOAL ACHIEVEMENT PARTNER

Top 20s also know they can increase their commitment to achieving goals through a Goal Achievement Partner. They know that their private, personal commitment to a goal can be stronger if they have a social commitment.

By simply telling a friend or parent your goal you establish a social commitment. It's not as easy to back away from your goal when you share it with someone else.

Furthermore, your Goal Achievement Partner might not only encourage you to stay motivated towards your goal, she might have some ideas or suggestions for achieving it. Top 20s are always open to receiving help. In fact, they often ask for it.

Bottom 80s tend to find people who **discourage** them from achieving goals. Top 20s attract goal partners who **encourage** them.

Remember: Goals are Dreams with Deadlines.

TIME FOR ACTION

1. Establish two SMART goals.
   - Relate one to a class in school
   - Relate the other to a relationship
2. Identify your commitment level for each goal.
3. What fears are stopping you from achieving your goals?
4. Develop an action plan for each goal. Who will be your Goal Achievement Partner? Check in with him once a week.

School Skills

During your teenage years, you are spending about one-third of your time in school or involved with school-related activities. Being able to successfully handle school responsibilities and concerns will greatly increase the quality of your ride as a teenager. This chapter will help you succeed in these areas by helping you to be **school smart**. Specifically, you will be more successful with school if you are more effective with homework, note taking and studying for tests.

Before jumping into a list of things to do to improve your homework and note taking, we want you to use The Frame first. Let's look at how Top 20s **see** homework and note taking.

First, doing homework and taking notes makes an impression on your teachers. Although you may not care about that, you should at least know that's how the game is played. It may not even be fair but that's life. There are some opinions your teachers will form of you based on if or how you do homework and take notes. You may be judged to be

- bright or responsible.
- lazy or half-hearted.
- dependable.
- unconcerned.

Like it or not, your homework is viewed as a reflection of you.

Second, if you didn't have an In the Moment realization yet, then homework is an opportunity for an After the Fact. If you didn't understand the math lesson while the teacher was presenting the material (ITM), then you need to get it later (ATF). Homework and taking notes might help you accomplish that.

Many students wonder why they should bother with the homework if they understood the material in class ITM. Well, Top 20s are concerned with **great** achievement. Take Mikhail Baryshnikov, the world famous dancer, as an example. Baryshnikov not only learns ITM, but he practices the same move over and over again ATF. Because of his dedication to "homework" and "study," his muscles are strong and flexible. Furthermore, he has created long-term muscle memory in his body enabling him to do the grand jeté and appear as if he is flying.

Your dedication to homework and study can strengthen your mental muscles and develop long-term memory which is what learning is really all about. Practice doesn't make perfect but it usually does make better. That's what Top 20s do. They get better.

THE DISHWASHER RULE

What do dishwashers get? Dishes. Yes, but what kind of dishes? Dirty dishes. Because they are dishwashers, they get dirty dishes. And what are they supposed to do with the dirty dishes? Just wash them.

What do firefighters get? Fire. Yes, because they are firefighters. What do receptionists get? Phone calls. Yes, because they are receptionists. What do dentists get? People with cavities. Yes, because they are dentists.

What do students get? Homework and studying. Yes, because you are students. Homework and studying are your pile of dirty dishes that need to be washed. So get your hands into the suds and do your job.

THE CHALLENGE OF HOMEWORK

You might consider homework as a challenge. Remember our earlier discussion on quitting, camping, or climbing the mountain? Think of homework as a mountain. Some students look at it and say, "Too hard (or too much). I quit." Others get started on the assignment but when it becomes more difficult they say, "This is getting too hard. I think I'll stop (camp) right here at problem #21." Top 20s, however, are energized by the challenge (climbing): "This is tough but I'm going to get it all done."

What's the result of quitting or camping? You get weaker. Top 20s are not interested in getting weaker. They want to get stronger—mentally, physically, emotionally and spiritually. Climbing helps them get stronger even if they fail to reach the top of the mountain. By facing the challenge, they get stronger and develop Star Qualities.

Which of the following frames about homework do you follow?

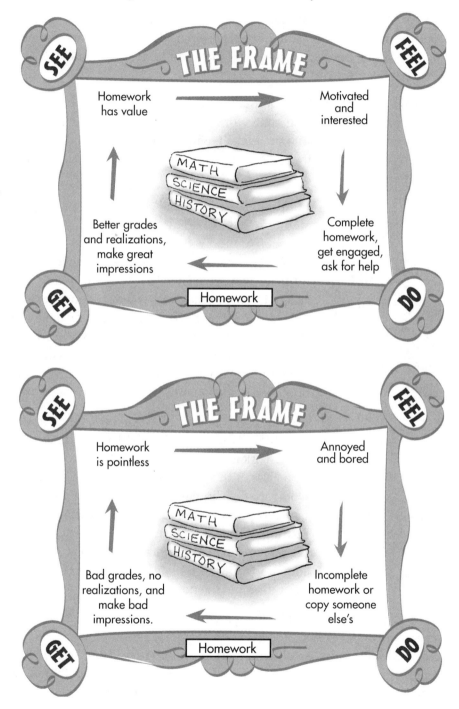

Following the Top 20 Frame is in your Best Interest. If you choose to go that route, the following homework and note taking tips can help you get better results.

HOMEWORK TIPS

Do Worst First: Do your worst homework first, the homework that you consider to be the most difficult or least enjoyable. Later, when you're tired, finish with the easiest. You will find that your homework time will be reduced if you try this tip.

Improve Your Study Environment: Being in bed in a dark room is helpful for sleeping but not doing homework. You will be much more effective doing your homework if you're in a well-lit room sitting at a desk. Have you ever noticed that there are more desks than beds in libraries? There's a reason for that.

Eliminate Distractions: What are you paying attention to while doing homework? If you're paying attention to the TV, then you're watching TV and not doing your homework. If you're paying attention to music playing on a CD, then you're listening to music and not doing homework. If you are going to do homework, turn off those things that distract you from paying attention to your homework. You will get your homework done in less time so you can do other things you enjoy. Plus, you will learn what your homework is all about.

"I learned how to do homework. Now when I go to my room I take away all of the objects that could distract me. I don't reach for the remote that turns on the TV. I turn on the lights so I can actually see what I'm writing. I found I got my homework done hours before I actually thought I'd finish. It was amazing. It made me do better on tests and quizzes and I got to do more stuff that I wanted to do."
– Angie

It's Not Just Reading: "Do you have any homework tonight?" "No, just reading." Many students think homework is only that which is to be turned in the next class or the next week. Writing is homework. Doing math is homework. Completing a science lab or an art project is homework. But reading is **just** reading. Wrong!!! **Reading is homework.** In fact, it's perhaps the most critical homework. It's not something that should go undone because you can't turn it in the next day.

Reading is a great way of learning and developing your mind. Do it when it's assigned. Better yet, do it even when it's not assigned. Unless you're writing a paper, almost all homework in college is reading. You are to read a number of assignments and are then tested on that material. If you haven't practiced this in high school, you're not going to be ready to play the reading game in college.

☑ **Consider the Five Levels when you have a reading assignment:** Have you ever read for twenty minutes without remembering anything. Why? You were never in The Zone. For twenty minutes you did My Life is on My Mind, Distraction, or Judgmental (page 105). You never did reading. Reading requires zoning in on the words in front of you. It's one of those things you will get better at with practice.

☑ **Short-Term/Long-Term:** If you're given a major assignment that's due two weeks from Tuesday, when do you do it? Many students would say two weeks from Monday. Considering that long-term assignments are worth more points, they should receive more effort. Manage massive projects by doing them step by step. Schedule the various parts of your long-term assignment on a calendar and "eat the elephant one bite at a time."

NOTE TAKING TIPS

☑ **Shrthd:** What does this mean? "Shorthand." That's one skill you want to develop as a note taker. Don't write out Minnesota or New York when MN or NY will do. Remember, notes aren't for your teacher; they're for you.

☑ **Highlight:** After class go over your notes and use a highlight marker on the five most important ideas covered by the teacher. It's instant studying and great preparation for later tests.

☑ **Numbers:** Look for any items numbered by your teacher. These are likely to be on the test. Example: What are the three different types of triangles?

☑ **On the Board:** If a teacher writes something on the board, you should write it in your notes. And if the teacher puts a box around it on the board, then you put a box around it in your notes. It's going to be on the test. Count on it.

☑ **First Five Minutes, Last Five Minutes**: These may be the most important times of any class. In the first five minutes your teacher is going to tell you what's going on in class that day. Pay attention and take notes. In the last five minutes your teacher might be summarizing what went on the last 40 minutes. Pay attention. Your teacher may also be telling you what your homework is for the next class. Pay attention and take notes.

☑ **Pretend It's Important:** If you believe that what the teacher is talking about is important, you will be a better note taker. If you believe it's not important, your mind will wander and no notes will be taken. So at the beginning of class send yourself a message: "What's going to happen in the next 50 minutes is important. I'm going to pay attention."

TWO STUDY METHODS: WHICH ONE WORKS?

Here's how some kids study for a test.

Example 1:

So neither of them studies very much for a math test that turns out to be difficult. How do you think the test went for Samuel and Zach? In hoping that the test would be easy, they "prepared" for an easy test. If they would have prepared for a hard test, they would have been ready for a hard test or an easy test.

Top 20s always ask, "**What if**...?"

"What if the test is hard?"
"What if it rains on the camping trip?"
"What if I can't get a ride home?"

In asking that "What if" questions, they tend to be better prepared for the challenges life often presents.

Example 2:

As they walk out of the test the next morning, Samuel and Zach agree that they were better prepared for what was a difficult test.

STUDY GROUPS

Study groups are extremely common in college and among juniors and seniors in high school. But the benefits of study groups are available to you right now.

• **First,** study groups can be a great social opportunity.

• **Second,** the language of study groups is student talk. That means that the material presented by the teacher will be discussed among students in a language that you might better understand.

• **Third,** strength lies in numbers. Sharing each other's ideas and notes will result in more complete understanding by everyone.

• **Fourth**, working with partners creates an energy to keep climbing even when the material becomes difficult.

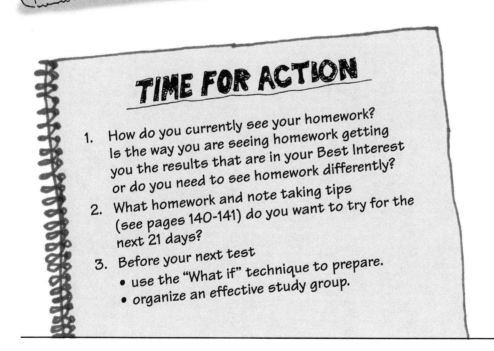

THINKING · LEARNING · COMMUNICATING

TIME FOR ACTION

1. How do you currently see your homework? Is the way you are seeing homework getting you the results that are in your Best Interest or do you need to see homework differently?

2. What homework and note taking tips (see pages 140-141) do you want to try for the next 21 days?

3. Before your next test
   • use the "What if" technique to prepare.
   • organize an effective study group.

COMMUNICATING
"PEOPLE-SMART"

People, people, people—they are all around you. You can't get away from them. You deal with people every day. As important as people and relationships are in your life, they can also be overwhelming at times. Yet, **the biggest influence on the quality of countless interactions you have with all these people is the way you think and act.**

Top 20s have **"people-smarts,"** the ability to build strong healthy relationships, restore those that need improvement and deal effectively with the conflict which is likely to occur in most relationships. You, too, can do this by developing your "people-smarts."

Like all teenagers, you have a strong desire to belong, to be a respected and accepted member of a group. "People-smarts" and your ability to communicate well will help you develop relationships with others that are mutually supportive and satisfying.

We want your relationships to provide you with whatever is in **your best interest** and others with whatever is in **their best interest**. With this in mind it is important to consider the influence you have on others and others have on you.

Along with what you have learned in the previous sections of this book, this section will give you some tools for building or restoring healthy relationships, relationships in which you are able to **discover and be your true self.**

Let your life be filled with great relationships!

Building Your Trust Fund

Without a doubt the most important ingredient in any relationship is **trust, the firm belief in the honesty and reliability of another person.** Top 20s understand this and know how to build and keep trust in their relationships.

Any relationship without trust will eventually crumble. The strongest and longest lasting relationships are those in which trust is abundant. Trust is fragile. Although you cannot build trust instantly, you can destroy it instantly. Therefore, it is important to create trust and protect it whenever you can.

Would you like your parents, friends or teachers to trust you more? This chapter is about making that happen.

THE TRUST FUND METAPHOR

In his book *The Seven Habits of Highly Effective People*, Stephen Covey presents the concept of the **Emotional Bank Account** to explain how trust is built or lost in a relationship. In working with our students in the TLC class, we have adapted this idea and call it the **Trust Fund**, a metaphor for building trust with people that operates like a savings account.

Example: Brittany worked last summer and deposited $1,500 in her savings account. At the end of the summer she withdrew $250 to buy some clothes and school supplies. So she now has $1,250 left in her savings account.

Like a savings account, we can make deposits to or take withdrawals from our Trust Fund. On the next page is a list of activities that are either deposits or withdrawals.

TRUST FUND

WITHDRAWALS DECREASE TRUST
- Being mean
- Lying
- Breaking promises
- Talking behind another's back
- Blaming or justifying

DEPOSITS INCREASE TRUST
- Being nice
- Telling the truth
- Keeping promises
- Speaking well of those who are absent
- Apologizing

One of the biggest benefits of having a high Trust Fund is that you will be able to resolve conflicts much quicker. The other person is more likely to give you the benefit of the doubt. Conflicts or disagreements are almost impossible to resolve if the fund is overdrawn. **Resolution requires trust.**

MAKING DEPOSITS

You may want to be making Trust Fund deposits, but may not know how to proceed. Here are five sure-fire ways to increase your account.

Being Nice: Anytime you are nice to someone you are depositing trust into that relationship. Random acts of kindness build trust in relationships. On the other hand, withdrawals occur when we are unkind.

NICE "DEPOSITS"	UNKIND "WITHDRAWALS"
• Saying "Thank you"	• Being sarcastic
• Hugging mom or dad; saying "I love you"	• Excluding or ignoring someone
• Smiling or saying hello as you pass someone in the hallway	• Ridiculing or laughing at someone
• Giving a sincere compliment	• Judging people based on appearance
• Introducing yourself to a new student	

Remember the tragedy at Columbine High School in Colorado? Reporters repeatedly described the two students responsible for the violence as loners. That means that throughout their school experience they had been picked on, made fun of, or ignored. This experience paired with their attraction to violent video games, movies, and music made them outsiders from the rest of the students and more likely to respond violently.

> "A girl in my class is very quiet and shy and seems unhappy. One day I saw her standing alone in the hall. I went up and began talking to her. Suddenly a smile appeared on her face and she didn't seem so lonely."
> – Andrea

We all do not feel the deep levels of loneliness and depression that were experienced by the Columbine students but, nonetheless, we all require frequent reminders that we matter to someone else. Those reminders can be delivered in all sorts of ways, big and small, but they are the essence of what being nice is all about. Could someone being nice have prevented the tragedy at Columbine? We'll never know.

TRUE TALES

When Willow was in high school she participated in the school play. During the weeks of rehearsal she got to know a lonely boy who was quite depressed. They got along well. But one day Willow noticed that he seemed to be overly depressed and was scared by the way he was behaving. She wrote on a note, "I don't know what you're thinking about doing but you're scaring me by the way you're acting. So don't do anything until you talk to me."

It turns out that this boy had been thinking about harming himself. But when he received the note, he shared it with his mother and his family was able to get him the help he needed.

Willow's concern for her classmate had a life-saving effect because the essential message through her note and the way she treated him during rehearsals was that he mattered; he was a person of worth and value. At a time in his life when he may not have felt that way himself, someone else did and that made a huge difference.

Telling the Truth: If you want to be trusted, you need to be trustworthy. **An absolute requirement of being trustworthy is telling the truth.** Lying or trying to deceive someone will always take huge withdrawals from your Trust Fund.

Keeping Promises: If you keep promises you are building a huge amount of trust. When you make a promise you build hope. When you keep a promise you build trust. Breaking promises are major trust withdrawals.

For instance, if you promise your parents to be home by 11:00 and come in at 10:55, you add trust to your relationship. But if you come in at 11:25, you have withdrawn trust.

When you give your word to someone you establish a bond. Keeping your word strengthens the bond and violating your word weakens the bond. **This is true even in your relationship with yourself.**

Speaking Well of Those Who Are Absent: When you Honor the Absent or speak well of someone who isn't present, you build trust with those who are present. They come to believe that you will speak well of them if they are not present. But if you Dishonor the Absent or speak negatively behind someone's back, you withdraw trust from those who hear you. They believe you will also dishonor them when they are absent.

Apologizing: No matter how hard you try not to, you are likely to say or do something that will offend even those people you care about most. If you apologize after offending someone, you restore trust. But even if the mistake was not intended and you refuse to apologize for wrong doing, you are withdrawing huge amounts of trust. **Remember that a sincere apology never has a "but" attached to it.**

WHAT'S IT WORTH?

The value of a deposit is determined by the receiver of the deposit, not the giver. Juan saying "I love you" to his mother will probably have a lot more value to her than his emptying the dishwasher. It doesn't matter how much value Juan places on the deposit. So find out what the high value deposits are for people who are important to you.

Any withdrawal of trust from a relationship is a serious matter. Depending on the severity of the withdrawal, numerous deposits are necessary to make up for the trust lost. One deposit does not necessarily equal the value of one withdrawal.

Taking the trash out three days in a row (deposit) in no way makes up for taking your parent's car without permission (withdrawal).

"I was in a little trouble because I wasn't getting up early enough to take the dog out. One morning I woke up extra early, took the dog for a walk, made a big breakfast and sat to talk with my mom. She really appreciated my effort in doing what I needed to do and taking more time to visit with her."
– Molly

One of our ninth grade students noticed **that you can get what you want and still lose what's important.** If you bug your mother incessantly for five dollars, she might give it to you just to get you off her back. However, your disrespect may have cost you a much larger withdrawal.

BUILDING TRUST WITH PARENTS

What you have just learned about the Trust Fund is important for building trust with anyone. In building trust with your parents, there's something else you need to understand.

Most of the things parents and kids argue about are Little Things, stuff like curfew, cleaning your room, doing homework or taking out the trash. These Little Things are important only because they are attached to Big Things.

Example: If you want to come home at 12:00 a.m. and your parents want you in at 11:00 p.m., midnight is a Little Thing. The Big Things are your desire for independence to make your own choices and your parents' need to know that you are safe.

THE BIG THINGS

Big Things are those things that are most important to us. If you and your parents help each other get the Big Things, your relationship will be smoother and more satisfying. If either of you doesn't get these Big Things, your relationship will be rocky and unsatisfying.

You understand the Big Thing for you: **Space**. It's important to find the balance between staying connected to your parents and having Space to be independent. You need Space to do your own thing and make your own decisions. You need Space to grow up and experience life beyond your own yard. This desire comes from deep inside you. You're wired for this. It's natural and necessary. It's simply called **freedom.**

Although you understand your Big Thing very well and your desire for it, you may not understand your parents' Big Thing: **Peace Of Mind (POM)**. To understand how your parents feel about you and your well-being, consider this example. Think of your most valuable possession (your tennis racket, your wallet, your favorite video game). How would you feel if that item were left outside in a parking lot for five hours this Saturday night? It could get wet, stolen or damaged. Would you be concerned with what might happen to it? That is the same feeling that your parents have when you leave the house on a weekend night!

> "After the Trust Fund talk I found myself tallying deposits. I tried to keep my account with my parents intact. I watch my balance very closely. You don't just make a deposit so you can make a withdrawal. You leave it in and let it gain interest so your balance or relationship grows."
> – Kelly

> "The Trust Fund was a huge realization for me. I washed my dishes after eating, cleaned up my room and tried to always be respectful. My parents were much more willing to do things for me, such as driving me places, letting me stay out later, and giving me more freedom. It really builds trust between us when I do what's expected of me."
> – Jim

In the minds of mothers and fathers, the two most important things for them come from their hanging on and letting go. Those two important things are your **safety** and your **growth**.

Parents need to hang on to best assure your safety and they need to let go to best assure your growth. When your parents feel that you are safe and growing, then your parents have Peace Of Mind. They understand this very well. It comes from deep inside them. They're wired for this. It's natural and necessary. It's simply called **parenting**.

THE LAW OF BIG THINGS

Teenagers need Space and parents need POM.
Parents give Space only when they have POM.
When parents give Space and teenagers handle that Space responsibly, parents have greater POM.
With greater POM, parents give more Space.

Breaking the Law of Big Things has consequences.

- If parents give Space and you don't handle it responsibly, parents lose POM and tend to limit Space.

- If parents don't give Space, you may tend to rebel. Rebellion reduces parents' POM and they tend to restrict Space even more.

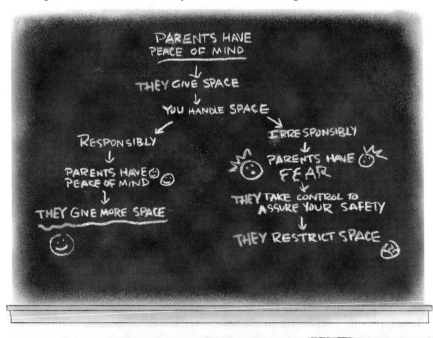

Some of the ways you can help your parents achieve Peace Of Mind is by

- getting home on time.

- letting them know where you're going and calling them if you go somewhere else.

- handling your school responsibilities.

- introducing your friends to your parents.

TRUE TALES

Tom's oldest sons both learned to drive under the Law of Big Things. After acquiring their licenses, the boys were given a two-mile radius of freedom in which they could drive the car: to school and back or to friends' homes. A few weeks later that radius was expanded to about five miles and included crossing the highway bridge to neighboring suburbs. By the time his sons were 17, Tom expanded the Space once again and the boys were allowed to drive throughout the entire city. This give-and-take gave Tom and his wife better POM and the boys more Space.

YOUR MISSION

There you have it. You can gain independence in one of two ways. You can create a revolutionary war or you can do whatever you can to maintain your parents' POM. Remember, there is a great deal of pain and suffering and numerous casualties in war. Choose Peace Of Mind and you will gain freedom without the misery plus a great relationship with your parents.

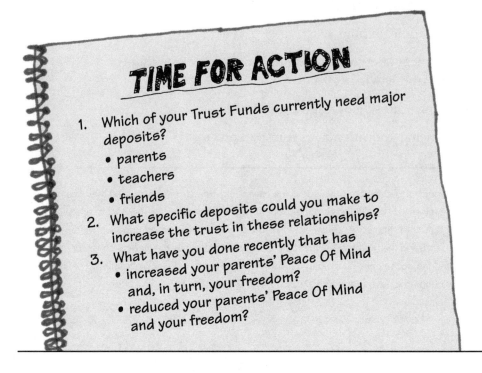

TIME FOR ACTION

1. Which of your Trust Funds currently need major deposits?
   - parents
   - teachers
   - friends

2. What specific deposits could you make to increase the trust in these relationships?

3. What have you done recently that has
   - increased your parents' Peace Of Mind and, in turn, your freedom?
   - reduced your parents' Peace Of Mind and your freedom?

"But I didn't say anything!"

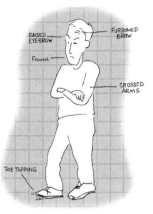

One of the most important things that human beings do is communicate. It is the primary way by which we connect with other people. However, as important as communication is, we're not always aware of **how, when** or **what** we are communicating.

NON-VERBAL AND EXTRA-VERBAL COMMUNICATION

Most people think that the primary way we communicate is by the words we say. We contend that only a small percent of what is communicated occurs verbally through the words we use (5%). Most of what we communicate occurs extra-verbally (30%) or nonverbally (65%).

Let's begin by understanding how we communicate in these three ways:

5% VERBAL: The words you use	30% EXTRA-VERBAL: The tone, volume, pitch or pace of your voice	65% NON-VERBAL: Your facial expressions, body posture, hand gestures; your dress, appearance and personal hygiene

WHAT YA GOTTA KNOW ABOUT COMMUNICATION

Countless books are written and numerous courses are taught about communication. So what we are going to talk about in this chapter is very important but only a small fraction of all that you should know about communication. Nonetheless, here are two things "ya gotta know."

1. You cannot "not" communicate

Even when you are saying nothing, you are communicating something. It's not a question of **if** you are communicating, it's only a question of **what** you are communicating. Inside our brains is a little voice that is constantly saying: "What are the people who are currently in my presence saying to me now?" Not only do we ask this question, we constantly answer it. Our answers may be wrong but they are the answers that we come up with when we "listen" to what people are saying to us.

But I didn't say anything!

2. You cannot "not" make an impression

The most important impression is the first impression, which people make within the first ten seconds of meeting you. This first impression is powerful because it is the only thing people know about you at that time. Consequently, they make up their mind about you based on that first meeting. Certainly correcting a negative first impression is harder than making a positive one. So it's worth remembering that **you don't get a second chance to make a first impression.**

THE DOG RULE

You can test non-verbal and extra-verbal communication with a dog. How would a dog respond to what we say?

Example 1:
What would a dog do if you said the following in a sweet, mild tone of voice with a reassuring smile on your face?

> Ohhhh, you bad dog, come on over here so I can cut off your paws and put them in the microwave.

Isn't it likely that the dog would come towards you no matter what words you use?

Example 2:
What would a dog do if you said the following in a gruff, angry tone of voice with a scowl on your face?

> Come here right now, my good doggy, so I can give you a delicious treat!!

Isn't it likely that the dog would cower away from you? The words don't mean a thing to the dog but the tone and body language communicate everything.

This may be surprising, but we are all a lot like dogs.

EXTRA-VERBAL: WATCH YOUR TONE

Words can be used to communicate different things. The same words can be taken as a compliment or as abuse. It's the non-verbals and extra verbals that make the difference.

Said with sarcasm by a student:	Said by a friend with a smile and sparkle in his eye:	Said by a boy standing too close to a girl at her locker and leering at her:

What's communicated? *"That's the ugliest sweater I've ever seen."*	What's communicated? *"I like your sweater."*	What's communicated? *"The sweater is not what I'm interested in."*

NON-VERBALS: ACTIONS SPEAK LOUDER THAN WORDS

In the classroom you are never invisible. You're constantly communicating to the teacher who is making judgments of you by what you do. Even when you don't speak, your non-verbal behaviors communicate loudly to people in your presence.

During the first week of class, Willow noticed Ellie, one of our TLC students, sitting in the back row with a mean and painful expression on her face. One day Willow approached Ellie after class and asked her why she was being so negative. Ellie responded that she loved the class and was fully engaged but that she couldn't see the board and was just squinting. Ellie was surprised to learn that her non-verbals didn't reflect her attitude. She started wearing her new glasses the following week and now both she and Willow are "seeing" things differently.

Be aware of the following negative non-verbals.

NON-VERBAL ACTION	WHAT IT SAYS TO OTHERS
Slouching	"I don't care."
Putting head down on the desk	"I am so bored."
Turning back away from teacher	"I'm not into this."
Doing history homework during math class	"History is more important than math."
Rolling eyes or smirking; walking away or door slamming	"I dismiss you. I reject you."
Making apathetic sounds: "tsk" or "hrumph," grunting	"Whatever. I don't care."
Doodling, pen chewing, desk drumming, foot tapping	"This is boring."
Looking at watch; sighing or yawning	"I'd rather be somewhere else."

"After TLC I tried to watch other people and their non-verbals. Our teacher gave more respect and attention to the kids that had good non-verbals."
– Matt

Although most students may not be trying to make that kind of impression, what does it look like from their teacher's perspective? The teacher has spent time preparing the lesson and the students' non-verbals are communicating that the lesson is worthless. You may not agree that this is fair, but it happens whether you agree with it or not.

Many times a teenager gets into trouble by what is communicated extra-verbally or non-verbally. His usual response is, "I didn't say anything." After reading this chapter you can see that **he communicated significantly even though he didn't say anything.**

"When I talk to my mom I don't roll my eyes nearly as often as I used to and our conversations now almost never end in arguments."
– Elissa

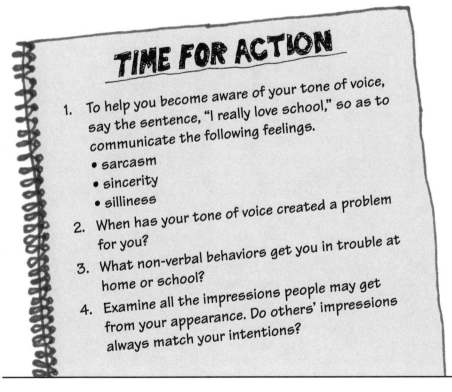

TIME FOR ACTION

1. To help you become aware of your tone of voice, say the sentence, "I really love school," so as to communicate the following feelings.
   - sarcasm
   - sincerity
   - silliness

2. When has your tone of voice created a problem for you?

3. What non-verbal behaviors get you in trouble at home or school?

4. Examine all the impressions people may get from your appearance. Do others' impressions always match your intentions?

Tornadoes of Negativity

Have you ever observed a tornado? Maybe you saw the movie *Twister* where the cow, fence and pick-up truck went flying across the road. The destructive force of a tornado occurs because of its tremendous energy that has a powerful vacuum cleaner effect wreaking havoc on everything in its path.

A person or group operating **Below The Line** or in the midst of a **Thought Circle** can produce a **Tornado**, **the invisible, awesome power of social influence towards negativity.** Sometimes their negative energy can draw an innocent bystander into the negative experience. In other words, when someone is BTL, she can bring someone else BTL. When someone is into a Thought Circle, he can draw someone else into that Thought Circle.

A dynamic of personal or group influence is that

- a positive person or group tends to influence others in positive ways.
- a negative person or group tends to influence others in negative ways.

HOW TORNADOES ARE FORMED

Our communication with other people is often an attempt to influence them or get their agreement or support. When we are communicating Below The Line or caught in a Thought Circle, our negativity is instantly contagious. As a second person is drawn into the conversation, a Tornado is spawned. The Tornado's negative energy now has the power to pull in a third or fourth unsuspecting victim. As it gets more and more intense, it tends to dominate the culture of the group.

A common response to someone's complaining is to express our understanding of what is being shared by adding our own complaining. This response may come from our need to connect, belong or be accepted ourselves.

The emotional drama in what Jake is saying draws Tim's response…

What will Brian experience when he comes to lunch Above The Line? That morning he got an A on a social studies quiz and received a favorable response when he asked Kari to go with him to the dance next weekend. Brian can sense the negative energy even before he sits down.

Jake continues his complaint:

The conversation between Jake and Tim has taken on the nature of a "spewing" contest where each participant "upchucks" negative energy on the other. Top 20s immediately recognize this phenomenon as a Tornado. Bottom 80s tend to get pulled in and add their own negative energy to the mix.

RESPONDING TO TORNADOES

We might like to carry a magic wand to wave over Tornado starters to get them to change. Unfortunately, such magic wands have not yet been invented. Although we can't tell you how you can change them, we can certainly tell you what you can do for yourself.

1. Identify the Tornado as such.

If you are approaching a group where a Tornado is being spawned, identify it as such: "Uh oh, sounds like there's a Tornado going on here."

After students in our class learned about how Tornadoes form, they became less vulnerable to being pulled into them. Once they were better able to spot Tornadoes, they were able to protect themselves.

Just like they do on the Weather Channel, it's important that you pay attention to Tornado watches, warnings and touchdowns.

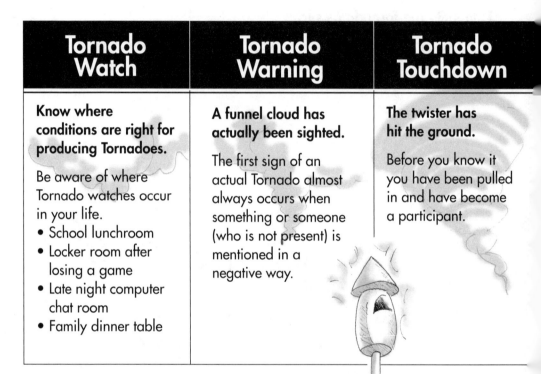

Tornado Watch	Tornado Warning	Tornado Touchdown
Know where conditions are right for producing Tornadoes. Be aware of where Tornado watches occur in your life. • School lunchroom • Locker room after losing a game • Late night computer chat room • Family dinner table	**A funnel cloud has actually been sighted.** The first sign of an actual Tornado almost always occurs when something or someone (who is not present) is mentioned in a negative way.	**The twister has hit the ground.** Before you know it you have been pulled in and have become a participant.

2. Listen without taking it to heart.

Learn the difference between listening to what someone is saying and taking what they are saying to heart. As soon as you take what they are saying to heart, you will go where they are. **It is possible to listen without agreeing.**

3. Respond by saying, "I hear you."

Jake and Tim both look at Brian as if to say, "It's your turn to rip on somebody." Brian feels the pressure and anticipates the social punishment that would come his way if he doesn't play along. What he would really like to share with his buddies is his good news: "Hey, guys, I've got a date for the dance Saturday night." But he knows that doing that will only direct Tim and Jake's wrath towards him.

Instead, Brian gives a Top 20 response to a Tornado:

By saying "I hear you," Brian acknowledges what his friends are experiencing without adding more negative energy to the Tornado. Furthermore, it prevents Brian from being drawn into the Tornado himself. He observes the Tornado but is not damaged by it. He observes his friends' situation but is neither affected by it nor victimizes others.

4. Leave the Tornado scene.

"I hear you" is a very effective response to a Tornado. However, if the Tornado persists with its "seek and destroy" mission, you may need to repeat "I hear you" a second time, or simply get up and walk away.

Remember, either by what you do or who you hang out with, you can develop the reputation of being a Tornado starter, of someone who rips on others. If so, people come to expect that of you. It becomes part of your identity within the group. Although you gain status by entertaining the group this way, it is not in your Best Interest.

5. Take more drastic measures.

Tornadoes are extremely dangerous. If certain friends or the group you hang out with are dominated by Tornadoes, you may need to take more drastic measures to protect yourself. You can do this by the **E-L-T** method: **Expanding** your friendships, **Limiting** your time with Tornado dominated groups, or **Terminating** some relationships.

Expand Your Friendships: Think about the number of people in your circle of friends. The fewer the number, the more influence those friends will have on you. You have fewer options. The more friends or groups you have, the less influence any particular group will have on you. You have more options.

The students responsible for the tragedy at Columbine High School in Colorado did not have multiple groups in their circle. Consequently, they were greatly influenced by the only group to which they belonged.

What could you do to expand the number in your circle of friends?
- Get involved in extracurriculars
- Make good impressions on other classmates
- Make a goal to meet three new people at school
- Make deposits in someone's Trust Fund
- Don't worry about Other People's Opinions

Limit Your Time: If certain friends in your life are having too much negative influence on you, limit the time you spend with them. Instead of spending two nights on the weekend with them, just spend one. A good way of limiting your availability is by making other plans.

TRUE TALES

Erin's story about talking to her friend is a reminder of how it takes courage to make any of these changes in your life.

"She was the popular girl in school; guys liked her, girls envied her. She would always boss people around and make people, including me, feel bad about themselves. It really annoyed me that she would consider me her best friend but then turn her back on me and act mean to me. I never got up the courage to tell her how I really felt about the situation so I went through seventh and eighth grade feeling this way. It got to the point where whenever I was angry at her I would take it out on my family.

"One day in TLC I realized I needed to spend less time with her and needed to develop the Star Quality of courage to tell her how I felt. I was nervous as heck the rest of the week but I knew that if I wanted to be a Top 20 I needed to expand out of my Comfort Zone and tell her the truth.

"On the way to see her my heart was practically jumping out of my chest. When we met I just started rattling on and on about my feelings for the past years and how the way she treated me hurt me a lot. She was a little shocked, probably because I had never done anything like that in my life."

Erin chose to openly limit her contact with her friend and, consequently, limit the influence. As difficult as this Top 20 decision was, it was certainly in Erin's Best Interest.

Terminate the Relationship: Sometimes it is necessary to actually end the relationship. When is it time to end it? You may have tried talking about the problem or you may have tried being a positive influence, but it's not getting any better. If this relationship is continually dragging you in the direction of your Worst Interest, it's time to terminate. Whenever a relationship is influencing you in a negative direction, it's time to consider ending the relationship.

Here's how you might handle the difficult task of termination:

Hey, I haven't seen you lately. What's up?

Listen, I'm not into the things we used to do. I've changed. I can't hang out with you anymore. It's too hard for me.

"This weekend I had to have a hard talk with my friends and terminate our relationships. I told them that I have changed and they haven't and that makes it hard to stay as close as we were last summer. They were hurt but realized that our friendship was never going to be the same."
– Anastasia

It might be easier to take it on yourself without blaming or accusing the other person.

IMPORTANT CLARIFICATION

Is what you have read about Tornadoes leaving you with the impression that you should never share negative feelings with friends or family members? That's not what we're trying to say.

In fact, we want to encourage the very opposite. We don't want you to stifle your emotions. We believe it is healthy to share feelings or concerns with others. When we conduct ourselves in this manner we are searching for another person's perspective and help. This is very different than feeling like we are victims and wanting others to affirm us in that role.

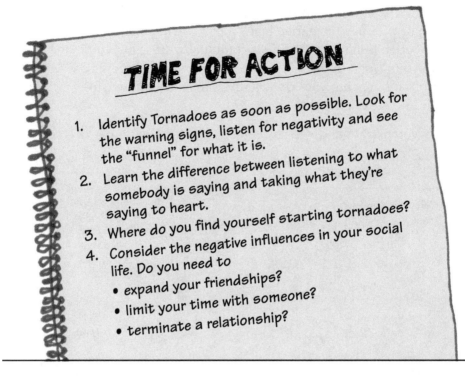

TIME FOR ACTION

1. Identify Tornadoes as soon as possible. Look for the warning signs, listen for negativity and see the "funnel" for what it is.

2. Learn the difference between listening to what somebody is saying and taking what they're saying to heart.

3. Where do you find yourself starting tornadoes?

4. Consider the negative influences in your social life. Do you need to
   - expand your friendships?
   - limit your time with someone?
   - terminate a relationship?

Responding to Hits

Hits are unexpected random negative events that can trigger a response or a reaction. They are the unseen potholes we encounter along the road that can knock us off course.

Examples of typical Hits include

- getting a surprisingly poor grade on a test or paper.
- being handed a note to report to the school office.
- being told "No" after you planned to do something.
- being dumped by a friend.
- being on the receiving end of a cruel joke.
- receiving a negative comment about your appearance.
- being cut from a team.

"Too bad we can't have an army officer speaking to us on an ear piece saying, 'Look out, cadet, here comes a big hit 100 paces north so be careful!' Unfortunately, life doesn't work like that. Hits like to lurk. They hide in the most unsuspecting places and come when you least suspect them."

– Maggie

How we see Hits causes us to feel something that evokes an action leading to an outcome (See-Feel-Do-Get). Unfortunately, these feelings are usually negative which leads to costly reactions.

FEELINGS FROM HITS		REACTIONS TO HITS	
• Angry	• Unappreciated	• Being defensive	• Seeking revenge
• Depressed	• Powerless	• Withdrawing	• Swearing
• Embarrassed	• Overwhelmed	• Being apathetic	• Fighting verbally
• Worried	• Stupid	• Attacking	or physically
• Humiliated	• Defeated	• Being sarcastic	• Crying
• Hurt	• Frustrated	• Sulking	• Backbiting

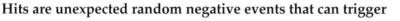

Responses or reactions to Hits can also be non-verbal facial expressions or gestures.

HOW TOP 20s AND BOTTOM 80s HANDLE HITS

Top 20s and Bottom 80s deal with Hits differently. As soon as Bottom 80s receive a Hit, they immediately react. Their reaction is based on emotional impulsivity. This usually creates a bigger mess.

Imagine that you're talking to a friend during a movie in a theater and someone sitting behind you says:

Now the mess has gotten even worse.

The Top 20s' first response to a Hit is to pause. Within this very brief pause they spontaneously ask the question, "What response is in my Best Interest long-term?" The answer to this question determines their next response.

The following diagram illustrates this difference between Top 20s and Bottom 80s.

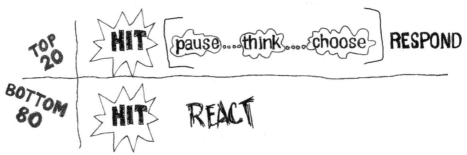

The Top 20s' response tends to move towards a satisfactory solution to the problem while Bottom 80s' response tends to create a second problem worse than the first.

PERSPECTIVE

Why do we overreact to Hits? Sometimes the perspective of the person receiving the Hit is different from the person delivering the Hit.

Let's look at three examples of Hit experiences and see how the kids perspective might be different from the adults.

Hit 1: A student walks into class after the bell and the teacher says, "You're late."

The student sees this as an attack in public.

The teacher sees it as simply informing the student of being unacceptably tardy unless the student has a valid excuse.

Hit 2: A player runs the wrong play during a basketball game and is taken out by the coach.

The player sees this as humiliation in front of a crowd.

The coach sees it as wanting to explain to a confused player how to run the play correctly.

Hit 3: A girl is about to leave for a dance in a tank top when her mother says, "Go back upstairs and take that off."

The daughter sees her mother as overprotecting and a control freak.

The mother is concerned about how her daughter might be judged by others if she's wearing a revealing tank top.

It's important to consider the difference in perspective during your Pause—Think—Choose time.

RESPONSE-ABILITY

"God doesn't have a list of people to give a bad day to."
– Kevin

Hits hurt. A common reaction to being Hit is to Hit back. Unfortunately, that's seldom in anyone's Best Interest. Top 20s have developed the habit of **response-ability** which is **the ability to choose a response to a hit that is in their Best Interest.**

Response-ability has two dimensions: Stability and Resiliency.

············ RESPONSE - ABILITY ············

STABILITY is the ability to take a Hit. Top 20s are more stable and better able to take a Hit without reacting in a negative way. Bottom 80s tend to rank low in stability and there is a cost to that.

+

RESILIENCY is the ability to bounce back after taking a Hit. Highly resilient people are able to get beyond the Hit and move on. People with low resilience relive the Hit over and over and hold on to the grudge forever.

Mr. Cody returned an algebra test to one of his students, Antonio. The test was graded "F." Antonio took the test from the teacher and loudly uttered a swear word. Tom scolded Antonio and offered him a second chance. The student crumpled the exam and tossed it over the teacher's shoulder. Antonio was then escorted to the Dean's office where he was able to think about three failures: one math test + two stability tests.

Five years ago, Mr. Cody removed Nellie from an all-school assembly. She and her friends were being disrespectful during a presentation, chatting for most of the hour. Nellie accepted the one-hour detention that Tom gave her (good stability) but her resiliency left a little bit to be desired. Five years later she met Tom in a local grocery store and made it clear to him that she still resented his actions at the assembly.

Antonio would have been better off if after he received his failed math test he said, "Wow, I really did poorly. Mr. Cody, what can I do to better understand this material?" Likewise, Nellie would be better off if she were more resilient: "It's done. I did my one-hour detention. I'm going to let go of this."

Why do Top 20s value stability and resiliency? With stability the problem doesn't escalate. If you are unstable and overreact, the problem will get worse. When you **react**, you give your power away or use it to make a mess. You will usually feel regret. When you **respond**, you use power to achieve something that is in your Best Interest. You will feel like you have control in your life. **Stability and resiliency help you respond in your own Best Interest.**

MY TURN

Another Top 20 way of looking at Hits is simply realizing that sometimes it will just be "your turn." Once in awhile

- the shopping cart in the parking lot scratches your car.
- the bird poop lands on your hat.
- the passing car splashes the puddle on your shoes.

Top 20s realize that Hits come with life and it's hard to be elegant under fire. So plan your responses to Hits ahead of time by practicing the Pause, Think, Choose technique.

> Guess it's my turn.

"February is always snowy and slushy and dark and cold. On top of it just being a terrible month, I broke my toe to start off the month. Then while playing basketball, I took an elbow in the face and got my front tooth knocked out. I could have gotten really upset, but I looked at the situation and said, 'I guess it's just my turn.'"
— Grant

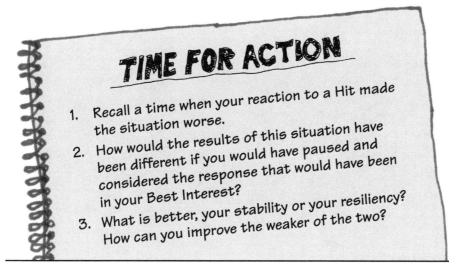

TIME FOR ACTION

1. Recall a time when your reaction to a Hit made the situation worse.
2. How would the results of this situation have been different if you would have paused and considered the response that would have been in your Best Interest?
3. What is better, your stability or your resiliency? How can you improve the weaker of the two?

Heart-to-Heart Conflict Resolution

Conflicts are fights, struggles, battles or clashes. Even though these are things we do not desire, they are common experiences we all have. Both Top 20s and Bottom 80s experience conflicts.

The Bottom 80s' style for dealing with conflict is **Toe-to-Toe.** This term comes from the sport of boxing and involves two boxers standing toe-to-toe while swinging at each other. Bottom 80s view the other person as an opponent and seek to win at the expense of someone else's losing.

The Top 20s' style is **Heart-to-Heart**. They seek a win for both themselves and the other person. They look for solutions that are mutually beneficial. They view the other person as a partner with whom they are searching for a better solution. The Top 20s' resolution also includes improving the relationship.

"Whenever I would get in a conflict with someone, I would try to go Toe-to-Toe, and usually I would lose. Now I use three strategies: win-win, listening, and using "I" statements instead of "You" statements. During an argument with my lab partner I just listened. Suddenly, I got a realization that he was actually right and that I was wrong. I ended the argument, saved time, and we weren't at each other's throats."
— Jim

Let's compare two ways to handle a conflict.

TOE-TO-TOE	CONFLICT RESOLUTION CHART	HEART-TO-HEART
I win—You lose	**SEE** (Intent or Goal)	I win—You win
Anger, defensiveness, frustration	**FEEL** (Emotions)	Willingness, respect, openness, cooperation
Working on it when we are unable to do it effectively (Below the Line)	**DO** (Actions or Behavior) **TIMING**	Working on it when it's most likely to be resolved (Above the Line)
My Life is on My Mind; Distracted; Judgmental; planning what to say while the other is speaking; interrupting	**LISTENING**	In the Zone; listening to understand; listening for the point; listening to non-verbals
Using "You" statements; debating, blaming	**TALKING**	Using "I" statements; describing problem without blaming; paraphrasing
Conflict is made worse or buried alive; resentment; Trust Fund withdrawal	**GET** (Results)	Relationship is improved; new and unexpected solutions; Trust Fund deposit

Listening and talking are two essential components of conflict resolution.

- Conflicts are often created or made worse by **ineffective** listening and talking.

- Conflicts are usually resolved or reduced by **effective** listening and talking.

"I came home late and was surprised to see that my mom had waited up. She did not have the nice mother face on but one of disgust. She began to yell at me and two words into her second sentence I stopped her. We both agreed that we would sleep on it and talk about it in the morning. The next morning she looked much more calm and collected and I was surprised when she only grounded me for the next three days."

– Pat

LISTENING: NARROWING THE GAP

WHAT'S BEING SAID))))))))))) WHAT'S BEING HEARD

When this gap exists, misunderstanding occurs. **At the heart of conflicts are misunderstandings** caused by poor communication between the two parties in the conflict. These misunderstandings must be eliminated before resolution can occur.

The only way the gap or misunderstandings can be reduced or eliminated is by listening to understand. This is best done by **reflective** listening that includes

- listening for content (what the words mean).
- listening for feelings (the feelings are being expressed nonverbally).
- paraphrasing (saying back to the speaker what she is saying and feeling).

The purpose of reflective listening is to gain understanding. If you don't reflect back the speaker's content and feeling, you may both think you understand each other when you actually don't. If you accurately reflect the speaker's content and feeling, the speaker will know she is understood. If you reflect content and feeling inaccurately, the speaker will correct the inaccuracy and understanding will more likely result.

Example: Your father is upset because you have come home 30 minutes later than expected.

Where are you now? The original problem has not been resolved and a bigger one has been created. You're grounded and the relationship with your dad is even more strained.

The mess has gotten messier.

Where are you now? You are now set up for conflict resolution. You and your dad are looking at a problem together. You have taken responsibility for your coming in late and are trying to do it better the next time. You listened and understood your father's perspective. In so doing he was then open t[o] listening to you. No misunderstandings exi[st]

The chances of resolving this conflict are now excellent.

TALKING

The second key part to conflict resolution is talking. What you say and how you say it will either help resolve the conflict or make it worse. Let's examine one effective response to resolving conflicts and nine ineffective responses.

"I" STATEMENTS

One thing that always makes a conflict worse is when people feel blamed or accused. The primary way this occurs is when "you" statements are used. "You" statements begin with the word 'you' and tend to point the finger at the other person.

The conflict can be better managed by using "I" statements. "I" statements take the focus off what we think the other person has done to us and reduces our tendency to blame. They help us identify our own feelings and, as a result, elicit a less defensive response from the other person.

"I" statements might follow this pattern:

I feel _____ when _____.

"YOU" STATEMENTS	"I" STATEMENTS
"You make me angry when you're not home on time."	"I worry when you're not home on time."
"You never help with the dishes."	"I feel it's unfair when I'm stuck doing the dishes by myself."
"You never listen to me."	"I feel ignored when I'm not listened to."
"You always decide what we're going to be doing."	"I feel left out when I'm not involved with deciding what we do."

> "'I' statements keep the communication channels more open."

NINE INEFFECTIVE RESPONSES

The following responses are sure to keep you Toe-to-Toe. They will keep you in the battle and increase the intensity of the conflict. Which of these are familiar to you either because you use them or the people with whom you are in conflict use them?

The Historian:
"I remember six years ago when you said…"

___

The Shrink:
"Your problem is that you take things too personally. You're paranoid. You make things up in your head."

___

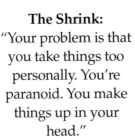

The Lawyer:
"That's not what I said. Maybe that's what you thought you heard but it's not what I meant. I can prove it. I have witnesses."

___

The Mind Reader:
"Oh, I know what you're thinking. I know what you're going to say next."

The Judge:
"You're dead wrong for saying that; thinking that; feeling that."

___

The Know It All:
"Let me tell you what you have to do. When I was your age this is what I did."

___

The Drill Sergeant:
"Stand right there and don't move when I'm talking to you!"

___

The Grammar Teacher
"It's not 'Me and my friend.' It's 'My friend and I'."

___

The Apathetic:
"Whatever! I don't care."

These are ways people use to win battles and they may be successful at doing so. What these common responses don't do is resolve conflict. In fact, they usually tend to increase the conflict or bury the conflict only to have it come back later with greater negative energy.

Be aware whenever you find yourself taking on one of these roles. They're indicators that you're moving towards greater confrontation rather than resolution. Eliminate these responses and your ability to resolve conflicts will immediately improve.

COMING CLOSER THROUGH CONFLICT

A student in our class had a serious conflict with her mother who disliked the girl's boyfriend. The mother wanted her daughter to drop the boyfriend and not bring him into their house. By the end of the year, the girl was still dating the same boy who was now being welcomed home by the mother. This occurred because of the way the girl approached her mother. The daughter followed the conflict resolution tips presented in this chapter and not only resolved the problem but strengthened her relationship with her mother. The mother was so overjoyed by what happened that she shared the following at one of our TLC parent seminars:

"A win in a win-lose situation is like putting a Band Aid on a bad cut that will soon be infected with anger and regret."
– Mark

> *"Our communication is so much better now. When we have a disagreement, we do the things my daughter learned in class. As strange as it might sound, it's actually good for us to disagree about things because we come out of them closer to each other. We've learned to focus on the real issues and to listen and understand each other."*

Coming closer is not only a desired result of conflict resolution but also a necessary part of the process. Usually in conflict situations the people involved see each other on opposite sides. This creates in them an adversarial mentality toward each other. As the picture portrays, when two people have a problem between them, they tend to see each other as the problem. This seldom leads to a satisfactory solution. Rather, it tends to make the problem worse and last longer.

It is much more effective in resolving conflict for the people involved to come closer, stand together and look at the problem side by side instead of face to face. By doing this they are more likely to see **the problem** as the problem and not **the other person** as the problem. They are more likely to work cooperatively at solving the problem rather than attacking each other. This way both people are on the **same side** trying to discover the best solution to the problem.

"One time my mom and I were both yelling and saying things we'd both regret later. I remember thinking to myself, 'Stop it, Cass. Nothing good is gonna come out of this.' I even told my mom she was going to regret what she was saying. She looked at me and I could tell she was thinking about what I had said. I could almost see the tears welling up in her eyes. It was one of those 'I'm sorry, I love you' type of looks. I know that we both got more out of that argument than what we were actually fighting about."
– Cassie

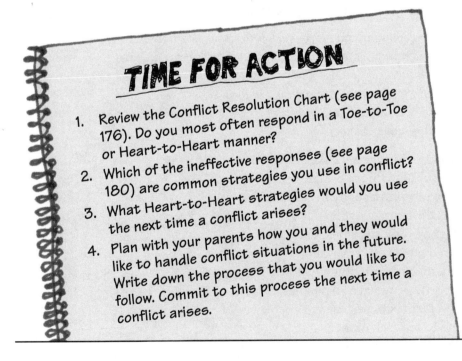

TIME FOR ACTION

1. Review the Conflict Resolution Chart (see page 176). Do you most often respond in a Toe-to-Toe or Heart-to-Heart manner?

2. Which of the ineffective responses (see page 180) are common strategies you use in conflict?

3. What Heart-to-Heart strategies would you use the next time a conflict arises?

4. Plan with your parents how you and they would like to handle conflict situations in the future. Write down the process that you would like to follow. Commit to this process the next time a conflict arises.

Instant Replay

Have you ever said something and then wished you could "catch" the words before they entered someone's ears? Unfortunately, we're not quick enough to "catch" the words but we can be wise enough to ask for an Instant Replay. Whenever we are having an unsatisfactory experience with another person, we can do an Instant Replay to make it better.

Top 20s desire and know how to make something better after they have made something worse. They use Instant Replays to get beyond a negative experience and feelings rather than being stuck in "yuck." They are then able to get on with life in a more satisfactory way.

The following story is an example of Instant Replay.

TAKE 1 . . .

As Paul returned home one night and got out of his car, he noticed that his daughter Katie had parked the family car across the street. The car windows were rolled down and the cloudy sky suggested rain might be coming. Paul remembered a week earlier when he got in the car one morning and his pants got wet. Someone had left the car window down the night before and rain had soaked the front seat.

With this in mind Paul walked towards his house. As he entered the front door, his wife and Katie were talking on the front porch. The following conversation ensued:

"Katie, are you home for the night or are you taking the car out again?" Paul asked.

"No, I'm home for the night."

"Will you roll up the car windows before you go to bed?"

Looking at her mother, Katie said in frustration, "Even he's on my case."

"What's that supposed to mean? All I'm asking," Paul replied, "is that you be responsible for using the car."

"I can't satisfy anyone," said Katie angrily.

"You're right. I'm not satisfied when I sit on a wet seat. So if you can't use the car responsibly, don't use it at all. In fact, don't use it for the next week."

With that Katie stormed off the porch and up the stairs to her bedroom.

CUT!!! Take two.

TAKE 2...

Paul sat on the porch upset by what had happened. After a few minutes of feeling crummy, he went to Katie's bedroom. The lights were off and she was already in bed.

"Katie, would you be willing to do an Instant Replay?"

"Yeah, dad, I think I would."

Katie returned to the porch as Paul went out to his car. He backed the car up ten feet and then drove forward parking the car in its original place. Getting out of the car, he noticed the family car with the windows down and remembered the time when his pants got wet. As he entered the porch Katie was sitting alone.

"Hi, honey, how was your day?"

"It's been a bummer, dad."

"I'm sorry to hear that. What happened?"

Katie shared with her father about the bad day she had experienced. When they finished their conversation, Paul said, "Are you going to be using the car later? I noticed the windows are rolled down and it looks like it might rain."

"No, dad, I'm home for the night but I'll roll up the windows. Thanks for reminding me."

When Katie returned from the car, Paul met her on the porch. He hugged her.

"I love you, Katie."

"I love you, too, dad."

"I'll see you in the morning."

The End

As Katie went off to bed, Paul sat on the porch grateful for Katie's willingness to do an Instant Replay. The crummy feeling and distance between them was gone. He felt close to a daughter he loved.

HOW INSTANT REPLAYS WORK

The reason Instant Replays work is because a realization has occurred. We approach the Instant Replay with a clearer sense of the big picture than we had originally. We see more completely.

When Paul first arrived at home, he didn't know that Katie had had a bad day and was Below The Line. He didn't know she was on edge. Katie didn't know the problem the windows being down a week before had caused. With this new knowledge and the desire to make things better between them, they were able to create a better experience through the Instant Replay.

If we are interacting with someone who isn't familiar with the term "Instant Replay," we can ask for an Instant Replay in other ways.

> *Example:* "I'd like what's happening between us to be better. Can we do this over again?"

> *Example:* "This hasn't gone the way I'd like it to. Can we start over?"

Sometimes we can do an Instant Replay immediately following the initial interaction. At other times it may be best to wait a few hours or a day before requesting the Instant Replay.

> *Example:* "Our discussion yesterday left me dissatisfied. I'd like to make it better. Can we run through that again?"

ALEX'S INTERVENTION

Alex, one of our TLC students, arrived home from school to discover that a full-scale battle had erupted in the kitchen between his sister and mother. His younger sister was demanding to have her haircut that evening; mom was telling her that it wouldn't be possible because her hair stylist wasn't available. The argument escalated to the point where both people were raising their voices and insulting each other.

Alex saw this as an opportunity for an Instant Replay. He could see that there was a big gap, a misunderstanding, that was causing the battle. He politely asked the two of them to start over and see if they could come to a better solution. His sister revealed a key piece of information that was missing the first time. She and her sixth grade friends had made a "pact" to all have their hair cut that same night. Once the mother was made aware of this critical point, she was willing to make an appointment with a different stylist. Alex had made a Top 20 intervention with an Instant Replay.

BARRIERS TO INSTANT REPLAYS

Fear and pride can get in the way of our even wanting to make things better. We may not ask for an Instant Replay for fear of being rejected. Our pride or need to be right may block us from improving a situation or relationship. After all, asking for an Instant Replay is an admission that we didn't do something right or as well as it could be done. A bit of humility is often required if we are going to make things better. It seems to be a principle of life that **when we know we are wrong we make fewer messes than when we think we are right.**

Another way to think of Instant Replays is as the delete button on your life's keyboard. If you say or do something that is a mistake, Instant Replays can delete what you said or did and replace them with words or actions that create something better.

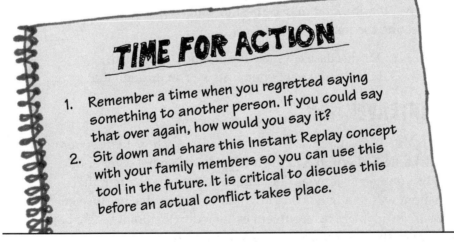

TIME FOR ACTION

1. Remember a time when you regretted saying something to another person. If you could say that over again, how would you say it?

2. Sit down and share this Instant Replay concept with your family members so you can use this tool in the future. It is critical to discuss this before an actual conflict takes place.

Feedback:
Staying on Course

Have you ever been off course?

An airplane flying from Minneapolis to Dallas is off course most of the time yet always ends up in Dallas. Why is that? It's because the pilot is constantly making adjustments to the flight of the airplane based on feedback from the control panel or the air traffic controllers in Minneapolis or Dallas. Without that feedback the plane could end up in New Orleans.

Like airplane pilots, Top 20s depend on **feedback: information that helps us to see how we're doing or where we're going.** They have people in their life functioning like air traffic controllers who might be aware of things the pilot's not seeing, like wind patterns, weather conditions, or the flight patterns of other planes. Top 20s are open to feedback from people who might be aware of things to avoid, changes to be made, or a better route to go. They might be aware that what a Top 20 is doing might not get the results she's seeking in her Best Interest.

If a pilot was not open to receiving feedback or rejected it when given, the plane would stray further off course and end up at the wrong destination. Likewise, Top 20s know their lives would get off course if they only depended on their own limited view of reality. Therefore, they **seek** feedback from their own personal air traffic controllers.

PERSONAL FEEDBACK

Top 20s are concerned with getting personal feedback. **Personal feedback is thoughts or opinions a person has about another and shares with her.** They want information on how to do something better.

Feedback comes in two varieties: affirming and critical. **Affirming feedback** says, "Don't change. You're doing fine. Keep it up." It feels good to receive affirming feedback and is easier to give than critical feedback. **Critical feedback** says, "Change. You have to do it differently or be different." We tend to be very open to receiving affirming feedback but defensive when receiving critical feedback.

REQUIREMENTS OF EFFECTIVE FEEDBACK

As important as critical feedback is, it is often not given effectively or received. The biggest cause of ineffective feedback is **defensiveness.** All critical feedback probably causes some level of defensiveness. Our challenge, whether giving or receiving feedback, is to keep defensiveness as low as possible. **This requires that the motive for the feedback be in the other person's Best Interest.** If feedback is not given with the Best Interest of the other in mind, you can be assured that defensiveness will be high.

GETTING FEEDBACK

Top 20s follow five steps in order to get feedback and make it meaningful to them.

1. **They ask for it.** Because Top 20s value feedback as a way to improve or not get too far off track, they ask others for feedback about how they're doing. These are people who are their personal air traffic controllers. They may include parents, teachers, coaches, friends or others who know them well. Top 20s know they are less likely to be defensive if they ask for feedback then if someone simply starts giving them critical feedback.

2. **They listen openly and are nonjudgmental.** As feedback is being given to them, they accept it as feedback on their actions but do not take it personally. They hear it as what they can do to improve and not that they are doing something wrong. They try not to agree or disagree with it at the moment but simply take it in. They receive the feedback.

Romeo, once more with feeling this time.

3. **They say it back.** In their own words they say to whomever is giving them feedback what they are hearing. This helps them receive the feedback as accurately as possible without creating a misunderstanding.

4. **They thank the person for giving them feedback.** Knowing how difficult it can be to give critical feedback, they thank the person for sharing the feedback. Expressing gratitude for the feedback will more likely assure that this person will be a source of feedback in the future.

5. **They decide on the value of the feedback.** They seriously consider how the feedback applies to them. They determine the parts of the feedback they will accept as important in helping them to grow. They also mentally discard portions of the feedback that are not applicable or in their Best Interest.

GIVING FEEDBACK

Giving affirmative feedback is enjoyable. Giving critical feedback is difficult. Fearing we might offend someone or have them mad, we often choose not to give feedback that could be extremely helpful to another. Top 20s practice five steps to make this challenging task effective and help minimize defensiveness.

1. **They communicate their sincere intent in trying to benefit the other:** "I care about you. I'd like to give you some feedback that might be helpful to you."

2. **They seek permission** to give the feedback: "Would you like to hear it?" They know that if the person gives permission, his defensiveness will be much lower. If the person says yes, they ask: "Would now be a good time?" If the answer is no, they know that giving the feedback would not be effective because of high defensiveness. They might say, "If there is ever a time you think you might want to hear it, let me know."

3. **They start by presenting the issue and listening to what the other person has to say about it.** Rather than saying, "I don't think you're studying enough," they would ask, "How do you see your study effort affecting your grades?"

4. **They then offer direct feedback.** After listening to what the other person has said, they share their thoughts or opinions: "Your decision not to turn in your homework assignments is creating a problem for you at school."

5. **They offer to problem solve:** "Do you want some help solving this problem?"

Giving someone critical feedback because we care about them may require that we step outside our Comfort Zone. When we do so we will benefit not only the other person but also develop Star Qualities in ourselves.

Like the flight from Minneapolis to Dallas, our lives are a journey made more successful when we receive affirming feedback and meaningful critical feedback. Feedback is what will get us there.

It's gonna be bumpy at 32,000 feet. Prepare for turbulence.

TIME FOR ACTION

1. In what area of your life do you see a need for getting feedback? Who are your personal air traffic controllers who could provide this for you? Take a chance and ask them for it.

2. Giving Critical Feedback:
   Is there someone you're concerned about who could benefit from your critical feedback? Consider how you could use the five steps (see page 189) for giving feedback to this person.

3. Consider someone who could benefit from your affirming feedback. What positive words could you share with them?

Leadership:
Creating Value for Others

As we near the end of our journey through TLC, you've now become familiar with several ideas that Top 20s use to better their own lives. They are always looking for opportunities to develop their Star Qualities; they are constantly striving for self-improvement. But here's the punch line: there is a higher calling for these Top 20s, for those people who have developed their TLC. **Top 20s look to lead others.**

In his book *Leadership from the Inside Out*, Kevin Cashman defines leadership as "authentic self-expression that creates value" for others. Top 20 leaders add something of value to the lives of other people. Think of people in your world that you consider to be leaders. Take a close look at the "value" that they have created, not only for themselves but for the other people around them. What Star Qualities do these leaders possess?

- Self-discipline
- Enthusiasm
- Courage
- Self-confidence
- Inspiration
- Optimism
- Organization
- Focus
- Trustworthiness
- Sensitivity

Top 20s use their Star Qualities to make a positive difference for others.

IT'S CONTAGIOUS!

Star Qualities and Negative Mental Habits are equally contagious. Leaders in any organization routinely exhibit these traits in their day-to-day operations. Any coach or manager who is bold or innovative will soon have a bold and innovative team working with her. Any foreman who is sarcastic and paranoid will soon find the same characteristics prevalent on his crew. Think about the groups, clubs or teams that you've been involved in; think about the type of leader you had. Did your group adopt the Star Qualities or Negative Mental Habits of that person?

Top 20 leaders with "self-smarts" and "people-smarts" are **germinators.** They think and communicate in ways that **foster the growth or improvement of others.** Leaders with high TLC tend to plant those small seeds of positive energy, nurture them, and watch them develop into deep-rooted, successful outcomes.

Leaders lacking "self-smarts" and "people-smarts" are **terminators.** They **limit or suffocate the development of others**. Whereas germinators help the group to flourish, terminators block potential and end what is possible in a group.

THE EQ FORMULA FOR LEADERS

Although a working knowledge of any vocation is required for a successful employee (firefighters must know how to use the hoses, administrative assistants must be able to operate a computer effectively), any successful career depends on a strong Emotional Quotient (TLC) as well. We believe that EQ is even more important for people involved in leadership positions. As with many other topics in this book, the 80/20 Rule can be applied here as well.

Leadership positions require 80% EQ and 20% IQ

Think about it. A successful high school principal does not need to be well-versed in chemistry, calculus or French. But she does need to be able to staff those courses with effective teachers. The CEO of a car manufacturing plant does not need to know how to build an engine. But he does need the "people-smarts" to build an organizational team that can get the job done. Simply put, strong leaders have the Emotional Intelligence necessary to put the right people in the right places, thus allowing them and the entire group to succeed.

INTERDEPENDENCE

THE LEADERSHIP CONTINUUM

As we grow from infancy to adulthood, there is a natural tendency to develop from **dependence to independence.** Top 20s become true leaders when they find a third level. **Interdependence is that higher state of being that creates value** for the group as well as the individual.

INTERDEPENDENCE
"We get what we need by working together."

INDEPENDENCE
"I get what I need for myself...
I am my own responsibility."

DEPENDENCE
"You get what I need for me...
and it's your fault if I don't get what I need."

INDEPENDENCE

DEPENDENCE

The dependent state is certainly an easy place to reside. However, the cost is fairly high. You are completely at the mercy of others, a victim of circumstance. While independence is much more fulfilling, there is still a feeling of selfishness and isolation. It might be a natural way to live, but it is not completely satisfying. Only in the interdependent state can we become our True Selves.

One great example of this principle involves Tony Rice, the quarterback of the Notre Dame football team in the early nineties. Rice had only above-average athletic skills, but it was his leadership ability that led his team to national prominence. Many of his teammates pointed to him as **a person who made every one on the team a better player.** Rice is an example of a germinator whose leadership added value to his team.

Like Tony Rice, Top 20 leaders not only seek to make themselves better but everyone better. You will know that you've truly become a Top 20 leader when you add value to the lives of other people.

We have witnessed many instances where our ninth-grade TLC students have chosen to use these Top 20 concepts in leadership roles. Chris taught the basic TLC concepts to his second-grade brother. Chris saw value in his own experience, then added that value to his younger brother's life. Another student, Bennie, built his own Frame and put it on his family's refrigerator. He saw benefit in the Frame's power, then brought that concept home to his parents and siblings. Bennie took his knowledge to the interdependent level, to that higher calling of **PASSING IT ON**.

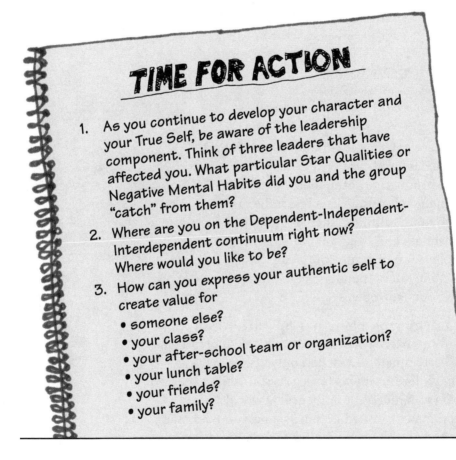

TIME FOR ACTION

1. As you continue to develop your character and your True Self, be aware of the leadership component. Think of three leaders that have affected you. What particular Star Qualities or Negative Mental Habits did you and the group "catch" from them?

2. Where are you on the Dependent-Independent-Interdependent continuum right now? Where would you like to be?

3. How can you express your authentic self to create value for
   - someone else?
   - your class?
   - your after-school team or organization?
   - your lunch table?
   - your friends?
   - your family?

PUTTING IT ALL TOGETHER

Everything that has been
shared with you in this book
is intended to promote your
life-long quest in becoming
your **True Self**. Once you
embark on that journey,
your life will explode in
marvelous ways...

Hangouts:
Core and Circumference

Take a look at the following list. What do all these places have in common?

- Park
- Tree House
- Gym
- Beach
- School
- Friend's House
- Youth Center
- Fast Food Restaurant

They're all places where young people hang out. Having a place to hang out is important. Where you hang out makes a difference in your life, relationships and experiences.

What we've really asked you to become aware of throughout *Top 20 Teens* is where you hang out. We're not talking about physical hangouts, but mental and emotional hangouts.

TOP 20 HANGOUTS	BOTTOM 80 HANGOUTS
Star Qualities	Negative Mental Habits
Above the Line	Below the Line
Curiosity	Blame
Self-Motivation	Procrastination
Honoring the Absent	Tornadoes
The Zone	Life on My Mind, Judgmental, Distraction
Beneficial Messages and Beliefs	Harmful Messages and Beliefs
Deposits	Withdrawals
Heart-to-Heart	Toe-to-Toe
Creating Value for Others	What's In It For Me?

Let's look at two more important hangouts in any person's life. In fact, they're probably the first two hangouts you ever experienced.

CORE: OUR TRUE SELF

Your very first hangout is your Core. This is where your True Self resides. You can think of your Core as what's inside a seed. What's inside a seed is the true identity and potential of the seed. What's inside your Core is the true identity and potential of YOU.

Seeds have worth and value because of what they are and can become. You, too, have worth and value because of who you are and what you can become.

An apple seed has a specific purpose, to become a tree that produces apples. Likewise, your Core has a specific purpose, to become YOU and share your unique gifts, talents and abilities with others. Just as the purpose of an apple seed is not to become an orange tree or a rosebush, neither is your purpose to become anyone other than who you are.

Did you get that? **You're not to become anyone other than who you are. You will never be happy unless you are becoming who you are.** An apple might admire the color of an orange or the scent of a rose, but it will utterly frustrate itself trying to become an orange or a rose.

Then why is it so hard to live out of our Core? Why is it so hard to know our true identity and potential, value who we are and be satisfied with becoming ourselves? The answer to that might be because of another place we commonly hang out.

CIRCUMFERENCE: THE LAND OF OP

As soon as you are born, you begin hanging out in a second place. This is the Circumference or the Land of OP – Other People. The Land of OP is full of wonderful and dangerous things. These often take the form of:

OPOs = Other Peoples' Opinions
OPEs = Other Peoples' Expectations
OPAs = Other Peoples' Agendas

Sometimes you become affected by Other Peoples' Opinions, Expectations and Agendas. They may want you to think or act or be a certain way…or not to think or act or be a certain way.

What's the danger? If you pay lots of attention to OPOs, OPEs and OPAs, you can forget your Core. You can forget your purpose of becoming your True Self. In fact, if you live only on the Circumference, you will believe that your purpose is to P.O.P. – Please Other People. You learn to please other people by satisfying **their** opinions, meeting **their** expectations and accomplishing **their** agendas. The more you do this the more you make a habit of pleasing other people or avoiding displeasing other people. The result of that is your unhappiness because you are not being yourself.

A powerful example of this occurs in the movie "Dead Poet's Society". Neil is the editor of his school's yearbook. When his father discovers this, he insists that Neil give up his work on the yearbook so he can focus more on his studies and get into medical school. Later, Neil gets a major part in the school play and discovers his passion for acting. After a wonderful performance by Neil, his father embarrasses him in front of his friends and withdraws him from the school where he had been discovering his Core.

Remember, there's nothing wrong with Pleasing Other People as long as you don't forget your Core or neglect your actual purpose of being your True Self.

Then what's wonderful about the Land of OP? What's wonderful is that we sometimes have an experience in the Land of OP that reminds us of our true identity, worth and purpose. Something or someone in the Land of OP may awaken in us the potential that is in our Core. Sometimes we meet people in the Land of OP whose OPO, OPE and OPA actually connect us to our Core. They want us to think, act or be according to our True Self…or not think, act or be according to our False Self. In other words, they see something true about our identity and potential. They value us for who we are and encourage us to be ourselves.

The movie "Lion King" offers a great example of this. Simba, a young lion, has developed the false belief that he is responsible for the death of his father. Steeped in guilt, he rejects his role as king and leaves his homeland. While living off by himself, he meets Rafiki, a monkey who sees the true identity and potential of Simba and guides him back to his True Self.

Because Bottom 80s are infected with Negative Mental Habits and False Beliefs, they are less likely to have a clear sense of their Core and are susceptible to the dangers of the Circumference. Top 20s, on the other hand, loaded with Star Qualities, have a clearer sense of their Core and are more likely to experience wonderful things on the Circumference.

YES OR NO

The quality of our life and relationships is impacted more by our choices than anything else. Our choices are the result of what we say YES to and what we say NO to.

It makes a difference where we are hanging out when we say YES or NO. Sometimes we say YES or NO from the Circumference; sometimes from our Core.

Bottom 80s more frequently say YES or NO from the Circumference. In doing so, they limit their potential and experience more stress and frustration because they are not being true to themselves. Top 20s more often say YES or NO from their Core. Consequently, they develop more of their potential and, by being true to themselves, experience more satisfaction and happiness.

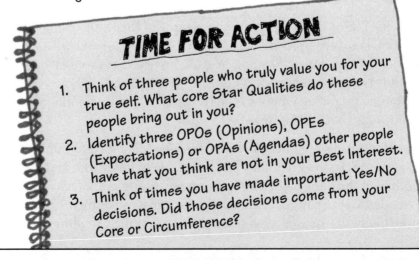

IT MAKES A DIFFERENCE IF WE:

Say YES to DFLIs (Don't Feel Like It), breaking promises or Thought Circles.

Or say YES to Instant Replay, using a Trampoline to get Above the Line or taking a healthy risk.

IT MAKES A DIFFERENCE IF WE:

Say NO to Life on My Mind, making decisions while Below the Line or False Messages and Beliefs.

Or say NO to feedback, Honoring the Absent or learning from mistakes.

TIME FOR ACTION

1. Think of three people who truly value you for your true self. What core Star Qualities do these people bring out in you?

2. Identify three OPOs (Opinions), OPEs (Expectations) or OPAs (Agendas) other people have that you think are not in your Best Interest.

3. Think of times you have made important Yes/No decisions. Did those decisions come from your Core or Circumference?

Becoming:
Quest For True Self

Whenever you do something it is important to ask the question: What's in it for me? By this we don't mean money, grades, awards or recognition. The more important result for you is **who you are becoming.**

MAGNETIC POWER

The principle of becoming is based on a natural law of life called the **Law of Attraction.**

> **The positive or negative results I have in my life are attracted to me by the person I have become.**

We don't necessarily chase success. Success is not something we reach out for. As if we were magnets, success in life is drawn to us by what we are becoming. This is true for failure as well as success.

Michael Cole was first exposed to the **Law of Attraction** in his mid-twenties. It started him on a life-long quest of becoming, a quest of discovering and developing his True Self. With his personal, financial, and professional life a total mess at the age of 25, Michael didn't get it when his teacher introduced him to this law.

"Michael," his teacher said, "**what you have at the moment you have attracted to yourself by the person you have become.** You have just said you are not happy with your job, you're not happy with your life, you're not happy with your financial situation. Whether you know it or not, you have attracted this to you by the person you have become up to now. If you want to change your life for the better, you have to stop trying to change all the things out there — like 'improving' your wife or kids or finding the right job. You need to work on you, on becoming a better thinker, learner, and communicator. I promise that your life will explode in positive ways that you never dreamt possible."

Michael took his teacher's lesson to heart. He swallowed it hook, line and sinker and today feels like one of the most fortunate people in the world.

BECOMING YOUR TRUE SELF

This book has exposed the secret tools of the Top 20 teens, those TLC concepts that separate them from the rest of the pack. Here's the bottom line: If you engage in the process of using these tools, you will **become** something wonderful: **your True Self.**

We all live in a material world where achievements and accomplishments are routinely celebrated. One of the big things that Top 20s all know is that **becoming is far more important than achieving or accomplishing.** They believe that by becoming their true selves, they will attract wonderful people and experiences into their life.

Bottom 80s think quite differently. They believe that their lives will be better only if people change or outside situations improve. The following are some examples of Bottom 80 thinking.

— "When my mother or father change or are nicer to me,
    then I will become a better daughter."

— "When my teacher makes the class more exciting,
    then I will become a better student."

— "When I find the right friend, then I will become happier."

Here's another big TLC secret of Top 20s:

- If you want a better **Parent**, then become a better **Daughter or Son.**
- If you want a better **Friendship**, then become a better **Friend.**
- If you want a better **Boss**, then become a better **Employee.**
- If you want a better **Sibling**, then become a better **Sister or Brother.**
- If you want a better **Team**, then become a better **Player.**
- If you want a better **Teacher**, then become a better **Student.**

By becoming better, you will attract better people or experiences to you. It's the **Law of Attraction**.

YOU DECIDE

It all comes down to making decisions... and it will be you making those decisions. It's time to face the crossroads that all Top 20s encounter. What do you want to "become"?

"After three months of TLC, I'm a different person. It's like what Dumbledore said in Harry Potter and the Chamber of Secrets, 'It's not our abilities, but the decisions we make that make us different.'"
– Pat

In order to do the work of becoming, you need to either become **more** or **less** of something. The following TLC topics might give you some suggestions.

IF YOU WANT TO BECOME MORE...	WORK TO BECOME LESS...
Aware of your thinking	Blind to your thinking
Directed by true beliefs	Misdirected by false beliefs
Filled with Star Qualities	Blocked by Negative Mental Habits
Responsible	Of a blamer
Empowered	Victimized
Of a healthy risk-taker	Stuck in comfort zone
Focused	Distracted
Open-minded	Judgmental
Courageous	Fearful
Of a "realization" learner	Of a "memorization" learner
Aware of hidden relevancy	Afflicted with boredom
Proactive	Likely to procrastinate
Goal-oriented	Impulsive
Responsive	Reactive
Effective in resolving conflict	Prone to creating messes
Adept at learning from mistakes	Likely to deny or dwell
Dedicated to the search for your true self	Adversely influenced by others' opinions

"TLC helped me look inside myself to find out who I am. I am still searching for myself and will probably always be searching, but TLC pushed me down the right path. If I keep following it, at the end of the road of self-discovery is my home, myself. I will become Nikki."

– Nikki

Remember that what you **become** is more important than what you **achieve**. Opt for the "more" column and you will become a better Thinker, Learner, and Communicator. You will become a difference maker, a Top 20!

It's all up to you now. Though there will always be supportive people with you, at the end of the day these choices are yours.

We hope you have enjoyed this ride with us. We've had an incredible journey together during the creation and teaching of the TLC material. Our most sincere hope for you is that you experience that same satisfaction, that same sense of self-discovery.

Have a great ride.

THE ~~END~~ *Beginning!*

P.S. You can email us at info@top20training.com if you have feedback or a TLC story that you'd like to share.

GLOSSARY

21-Day Rule   practicing a new behavior for 21 days so it becomes a behavior [122]

80/20 Rule   states that 20% of the people in any group or organization make 80% of the impact or the difference [3]

90/10   a Top 20 belief that most (90%) of our success or experience is influenced by our thinking or inside world and very little (10%) is caused by outside conditions [21]

Above The Line (ATL)   viewing life in such a way that our thinking serves us well [45]

Absent Shield   a metaphor for avoiding responsibility after Missing the Boat [125]

After the Fact (ATF)   an understanding of material after it has been presented [115]

Belief   an idea that someone thinks is true [37]

Best Interest   that which is a true and lasting benefit for us [78]

Blame-thrower   a symbol for our tendency to blame others and not take responsibility. [24]

Bottom 80   that group of people who have little effect on their lives because they have not developed or do not use the Thinking, Learning or Communication tools of the Top 20. [3]

Below The Line (BTL)   viewing life in such a way that our thinking is not in our Best Interest [45]

Burning Match   a metaphor for hanging on to false beliefs or messages [63]

Circumference/Land of OP   the "hangout" in our life where we experience Other People's expectations, opinions or agendas [198]

Comfort Zone   the place where people feel safe, predictable and in control [73]

Conviction Scale   a tool that measures strength of belief [39]

Core   the "hangout" in our life where we experience our true self—worth, purpose and potential [198]

Deposit   a positive contribution to the Trust Fund [147]

DFLI (Don't Feel Like It)   a justification for procrastination [102]

Dishonor the Absent   badmouthing someone who is not present [150]

Dishwasher Rule   a metaphor that means "it comes with the turf" [138]

Distracted   level three listening by which we give our attention to something in our environment [108]

Dog Rule   the canine test that demonstrates the power of extra-verbal and non-verbal communication [156]

DWANNA (Don't WANNA)   a justification for procrastination [102]

Ease-Up   a technique for lowering your conviction of a false belief or Negative Mental Habit [40]

E-L-T Responses   making changes with peer relationships by either Expanding, Limiting or Terminating [165]

EQ (Emotional Quotient)   the degree to which a person has Thinking (self-smarts), Learning (school-smarts) or Communicating (people-smarts) skills [12]

Excuse Shield   a metaphor for using excuses to deflect responsibility. [25]

Facts   that which is true for all people [37]

Fade   the tendency for our well-intended behavior to revert back to former habits [122]

Feedback   information from others that might help us see how we are doing or where we are going [187]

Frame, The   the See-Feel-Do-Get metaphor that can be applied to all situations and circumstances to achieve desired results [15]

Good Results   desired outcomes [11]

Good Ride   positive or meaningful experiences [11]

Heart-to-Heart   the Top 20s' approach to conflict resolution which seeks benefit for both people [175]

Hits   unexpected, random negative events that happen to us [169]

Honor the Absent   speaking well of someone who is not present [150]

Indicators   feelings or reactions that alert us that we are Below The Line [48]

Influence   subtle power that changes the thinking or action of another person [64]

Intellectual Muscle (IM)   the mental strength needed for solving our problems [88]

Instant Replay   doing a conflict or problem situation over again in order to produce better results [183]

IQ (Intelligence Quotient)   Book smarts [11]

In the Moment (ITM)   an immediate understanding of the material as it is being presented [115]

IUTGAWI (I Used To Get Away With It)   a classic justification for procrastination [100]

Judgmental   level two listening by which we like or dislike, agree or disagree, with someone or something [107]

Law of Attraction   the positive or negative results we have in our life are attracted to us by the person we have become [201]

Law of Beliefs   whatever it is we believe is real for us [37]

Law of Big Things   when parents give Space and teens handle that Space responsibly, parents have greater Peace of Mind and give more Space [148]

Law of Conviction   the more we believe something to be true,
the more real it is for us [39]

Law of "I AM"   whatever we say after we say "I am..." is what we will become [38]

Law of Mental Habits   by eliminating or reducing a negative
mental habit, positive mental habits will grow and flourish [93]

Leadership   creating value for others [191]

Levels of Commitment   degree of dedication to achieving a goal
symbolized by Quitting, Camping or Climbing [134]

Line, The   a metaphor for understanding our state of mind, moods or attitudes
as being Above The Line or Below The Line [45]

Messages   powerful true or false statements that are communicated to us from others
that influence our beliefs [59]

Missing the Boat   missing out on something we would benefit from if we were
present [123]

My Life Is On My Mind   level one listening by which we concentrate our focus on our
world [105]

My Turn   the attitude enabling us to not take Hits personally [173]

Name, Claim and Tame   a technique for dealing with problems by clearly identifying
them (Name), accepting responsibility for them (Claim), and doing something to
solve them (Tame) [94]

Negative Mental Habits   attitudes or ways of thinking that block our success [93]

Not Now   a technique used to eliminate distractions or negative thoughts.[56]

OPOs (Other Peoples' Opinions)   an outside influence on our thinking or actions which is
really none of our business [79]

Paradigms   the patterned way we see reality; they may be correct or incorrect
but are always incomplete [30]

Parking Lot   a metaphor for temporarily storing distracting thoughts [56]

Pat's Rule   reframing an activity we are not motivated to do into an activity we
are motivated to do [23]

Peace Of Mind (POM)   a parents' feeling of well being when kids are safe [151]

People-Smart   the ability to build strong healthy relationships, restore those
that need improvement and deal effectively with the conflict which is
likely to occur in most relationships [11-12]

Piccolo, The   an analogy used to describe the beginning stages of boredom [97]

Plywood Rule, The   an organizational metaphor that illustrates taking action
before, during or after an upcoming event [120]

Processing   level four listening by which we concentrate on analyzing, memorizing or synthesizing [109]

Quit-Camp-Climb   the three-level metaphor for commitment to a goal [135]

Realizations   the ultimate goal of learning; meaningful, deeper understanding [113]

Resiliency   the ability to bounce back after taking a Hit [172]

School-Smart   the ability to experience learning as a relevant activity with meaningful results [11-12]

Self-Smart   the ability to be aware of the power within you to control your life and make choices in your Best Interest [11-12]

SMART (Specific, Measurable, Action oriented, Realistic, Time limited)   effective goal setting steps [130-132]

Space   freedom and independence [151]

Stability   the ability to take a Hit gracefully [172]

Star Qualities   personal strengths or positive characteristics [7]

Submarine   a metaphor for maintaining dignity and protecting ourselves and others when we go Below The Line [48]

Success Formula, The (S = EQ x IQ)   our success in life is a function of our Emotional Quotient (self-, school- and people-smarts) and our Intelligence Quotient (book-smarts) [12]

Thought Circles   negative thought patterns that develop rapidly and are likely to occur when we are Below The Line [53]

TLC   Thinking, Learning and Communicating [4]

Toe-to-Toe   Bottom 80s' approach to conflict resolution which results in a benefit for one and a loss for the other [175]

Top 20   that group of people who make a major difference in their lives, relationships and experiences because they have developed and use the Thinking, Learning and Communication tools presented in this book [3]

Tornado   the invisible, destructive power of negative social influence [161]

Trampolines   a way we can rebound from Below The Line to Above The Line [49]

Triggers   those conditions influencing us to go Below The Line.[49]

Trust Fund   a savings account metaphor that measures the health of a relationship [147]

What if?   a technique that better prepares us for a situation by considering in advance what might happen [142]

What's In It For Me?   a question we ask to determine relevancy for ourselves [87]

WISE (Will-power, Initiative, Stamina, Enthusiasm)   indicators of persistence in achieving goals [135]

Withdrawal   a negative act that diminishes the Trust Fund [147]

Yet   an attitude that motivates us to learn After The Fact when we haven't learned In The Moment [116]

Zone, The   level five listening by which we are totally present in the moment to what we are experiencing [110]

BIBLIOGRAPHY

Barker, Joel A. (1992). *Future Edge; Discovering the New Paradigms of Success.* New York, NY: William Morrow and Company Inc.

Bryce, Ian and Kennedy, Kathleen (Producers), De Bont, Jan (Director) (1996). *Twister* (Motion Picture), United States: Warner Brothers Studios.

Cashman, Kevin (1999). *Leadership From the Inside Out: Becoming a Leader for Life.* Provo, UT: Executive Excellence Publishing.

Covey, Stephen R. (1989). *The 7 Habits of Highly Effective People.* New York, NY: Simon and Schuster.

Frankl, Victor E. (1962, 1963). *Man's Search for Meaning.* Boston, MA: Beacon Press.

Glasser, William (1998). *Choice Theory: A New Psychology of Personal Freedom.* New York, NY: Harper-Collins.

Goleman, Daniel (1995). *Emotional Intelligence: Why It Can Matter More Than IQ.* New York, NY: Bantam Books.

Haft, Steven (Producer), Weir, Peter (Director) (1989). *Dead Poets Society* (Motion Picture), United States: Touchstone Pictures.

Hahn, Don (Producer), Allers, Roger and Minkoff, Rob (Directors) (1994). *Lion King* (Motion Picture), United States: Walt Disney Pictures.

Kuhn, Thomas S. (1970). *The Structure of Scientific Revolutions.* Chicago, IL: University of Chicago Press.

Mehrabian, Albert (1971). *Silent Messages.* Belmont, CA: Wadsworth.

Mehrabian, Albert (1972). *Nonverbal Communication.* Chicago, IL: Aldine Atherton.

Pransky, George S. (1991). *The Relationship Handbook: A Simple Guide to More Satisfying Relationships.* New York, NY: McGraw-Hill.

Satir, Virginia (1972). *Peoplemaking.* Palo Alto, CA: Science and Behavior Books, Inc.

Stoltz, Paul G. (1997, 1999). *Adversity Quotient – Turning Obstacles into Opportunities.* New York, NY: John Wiley and Sons, Inc.

TOP 20 TRAINING
PROVIDES TRAINING AND MATERIALS
TO EMPOWER YOUTH AND ADULTS

- to develop their potential
- to make a positive difference in their lives, relationships and experiences
- to make a positive difference in the lives of others

Top 20 training sessions: Top 20 training sessions are conducted for youth, educators, parents, coaches, social workers and other adults working in a wide variety of businesses, churches and organizations. For a schedule of Top 20 training sessions, go to www.top20training.com. To schedule a training session for your school or organization, contact Top 20 Training at info@top20training.com.

Top 20 books: *Top 20 Teens: Discovering the Best-kept Thinking, Learning & Communicating Secrets of Successful Teenagers*

Top 20 Parents: Raising Happy, Responsible and Emotionally Healthy Children

Top 20 teachers manuals: Teacher manuals include Top 20 classroom processes, detailed lesson plans for all concepts in the Top 20 Teens book and a handout for students.

Top 20 TLC Teacher Manual: for grades 3-6
Top 20 Teens Teacher Manual: for grades 7-12

If you have questions about Top 20 Training or would like to order books or materials, contact top 20 Training.

www.top20training.com   info@top20training.com   651-690-5758